Yes, You Can Afford Disney!

Hundreds of Practical Tips for Planning and Affording the Disney Vacation of Your Dreams

By Michelle Crawford

The text of this book was set in Book Antiqua.
First Edition September 2016

Dedicated to my husband Adam, who is my prince charming; to my darling daughter Molly, a strong and beautiful princess; and my sweet son Will, who would love nothing better than to spend all day on the monorail.

Acknowledgments

Many thanks to my family and friends for helping me write and edit this book, especially Sarah and Rita for answering my proofreading questions.

Table of Contents

List of Pictures and Figures

Preface: Can I Afford Disney?

If you're reading this book, chances are you've asked that question. Maybe you want to take your family (and especially your children) on their dream vacation to Disney World, but have always assumed it would break the bank. Perhaps you went to Disney's website, looked at their ticket and hotel prices, got discouraged, and gave up. While it's true that the only ways to have a completely free vacation are to win a contest or to be gifted one by a wealthy friend or relative, I've assembled some easy strategies that may put a Disney vacation back within reach.

This book assumes you have regular internet access. It's also helpful to have a smartphone or smart device where you can download and run apps. (If you don't, you may want to consider buying a cheap "go-phone" you can use on Wi-Fi solely for the purpose of running apps.) I've included web addresses and further resources throughout the chapters where you can go for more information. All websites can also be found in the appendix. While they were up-to-date at the time of writing, the web is a very fluid place where addresses can change overnight without warning; therefore, if I happen to send you to a broken link, don't despair. You can probably find the updated link by putting the web page title into Google and doing a search.

I'm also assuming you have some sort of income, however small, and are not so far in debt that you shouldn't take any vacations, much less one to Disney. I'm not going to advocate going into debt for a vacation. In the big picture of life, vacations are a "want," not a "need," and if you can't pay your rent, you probably shouldn't be considering a vacation. I feel positive, though, that you're reading this book because you *don't* want to go into debt to afford a fantastic vacation. Whatever your situation, prioritizing your vacation is a personal matter and should be left to your own consideration in the end. You know your family's finances best. That said, it's possible to put these strategies to use for paying down debt and making that Disney vacation your goal after a few years of savings.

The secret to affording a Disney vacation is planning, planning, and more planning. That's why the first several chapters of this book are devoted to establishing a budget and saving money before you ever leave home. Toward the end of this book we'll cover keeping your Disney experience affordable and within your budget while you're on your vacation, without skimping on fun. Of course, using the tips in the first part of the book, it's possible to budget for a vacation that doesn't require saving money while you're on it! The sky's the limit.

As you read this book, please don't think you have to read it cover-to-cover. Some chapters may apply to you, some may not. You may have already established a budget but need to figure out how to save money while on your vacation, in which case you should skip the first part of the book entirely. Jump around from chapter to chapter, or read from front to back; approach this book however best you think it will help you and your family.

You'll also notice that I have written this book with a focus on Walt Disney World in Orlando, Florida. I have been a Florida resident for nearly thirty years and have never been to Disneyland in California, so it's only natural that I would have a bias for the park in my home state. That said, I feel confident that families looking to afford a Disneyland vacation will also get plenty of good information out of this guide.

Now, let's go ahead and get to the business of reaching for the stars and making dreams come true by putting that Disney vacation within reach.

Chapter 1: Establishing a Household Budget

Are you overwhelmed by the idea of paying for a Disney vacation, and aren't sure where to start? The first place you'll need to start is by budgeting. First, establish a household budget, and see exactly how much you're spending, and where. If you already have a household budget, good for you! You can skip ahead to the next chapter.

Many people use specialized software they've purchased, like Quicken, to establish a household budget. This works, but I assure you it isn't necessary. If you have Microsoft Office, you can use Excel to establish and track a budget. This is what my family does. My husband is an Excel programmer and has created an elaborate budget spreadsheet containing multiple tabs and automatic calculations. It automatically projects our spending so that we can see where and when we need to cut back. Now, this book isn't an Excel guide, so I won't be going into that, but I also want to emphasize that it isn't necessary to get down to that level of detail. It's easy to start from scratch and create a basic budget without a lot of bells and whistles that can help you keep track of your money.

Don't have Microsoft Office and don't want to pay for it? No problem. There are completely free, open-source software suites available that do the same thing. One is called OpenOffice and contains a program called Calc that has all the same features as Excel. Another is LibreOffice. Its spreadsheet application is also called Calc.

There are even apps that can help you establish a budget. Mint, Mvelopes, and You Need A Budget (YNAB) are all examples.

Let's start by figuring out your income. List all your sources of income in the spreadsheet and add them all up. Don't forget hidden sources outside of your paycheck, such as child support, bank account interest, tips, bonuses, tax refunds, regular gifts, and dividends.

Next, list all your expenses. Start with the easy ones, like your monthly rent or mortgage, electric bill, water bill, gas bill, cable bill, loan payments, car payments, etc. Look for expenses that occur regularly on a month-to-month basis. Don't forget regular expenses that may occur quarterly or annually, like taxes, school fees, birthday and Christmas gifts, membership dues, or homeowners' association fees. After you've listed your regular expenses, have a look at what you spend on things like food, gas, and entertainment. Try to look at these expenditures over time and develop a rough estimate of what your average spending is. Break down your food expenses between groceries and restaurants so you can see what you're spending on each category.

Yes, this will take some time and effort, but it is well worth it. You may be surprised at where your money is going. You may even be shocked, depressed, or upset. But if you are determined to afford a Disney vacation, don't be discouraged. This is only a place to start. Today is a new day and a new focus on your goal.

Chapter 2: Establish a Disney Budget Goal

Let's set aside the household budget for the moment. We'll come back to it later. Now is the time to really start dreaming. What kind of Disney vacation do you really want to take? The point of this exercise is to figure out exactly how much you will need to set aside to afford the Disney vacation of your dreams.

It's okay to dream big, but try to keep it a little bit realistic – we'd all like to stay at the Cinderella Castle suite inside the Magic Kingdom, but that isn't even open to the public! It would also be nice to stay in a Presidential suite in one of the monorail hotels, but that is probably out of the price range of most of us ordinary people. If you realistically think you will be able to save up for the $1,000-$2,500 a night it would cost just for the accommodations, though, go ahead and put that down on your list!

This is another place an Excel or Calc spreadsheet will come in handy. Open a spreadsheet now and be ready to put in all the expenses you think you might need to account for on your Disney trip.

The most basic questions to ask yourself will be: how many nights do we want to spend on our vacation, how will we get there and back, and what kind of hotel do we want to stay at? Let's break down these questions one-by-one. The first question is easier than the other two, so we'll break those out into the next chapter.

How many nights do we want to spend on our vacation?

Think carefully about this. It would be awesome to spend two weeks at Disney, wouldn't it? But is that really practical? Think about how much time you can get off work, what time of year you want to go, whether you want to pull the kids out of school or whether you plan to go over a major holiday. A week is probably a good, realistic time frame, but it's also very possible to spend just a few days there and have a wonderful time. Also consider that a shorter stay will be more affordable, but would you perhaps be willing to put off your Disney vacation for a year or two in order to save up for a longer trip? What are your "must-dos" when you are at Disney? How much time will you need in order to see and do everything on your wish list? Go to the Disney website and the other planning sources listed in the appendix and start narrowing it down.

Chapter 3: Budgeting for Transportation and Lodging

The next few basic questions require a little more thought, and a little more calculation.

How will we get there and back?

First, consider flying. How much are airline tickets? How many people are in your family? Just for an idea, you can go to an airline price-compare website like Kayak and input your flight plan and the number of people to get a rough idea of how much airline tickets are going for right now. If you don't know the dates you'd like to go yet, just take a guess at the time of year you might consider going. Find a representative flight cost and put that in your spreadsheet. Do you have any airline miles you can redeem toward the flights? Don't forget that websites like Kayak won't include discount carriers like Southwest and Spirit – you'll have to look at the individual websites for those carriers and repeat this exercise for them. Also consider any extra fees the airlines will charge, like checked baggage fees, frequently $25 per bag.

If you're determined to fly but don't want to pay very much, you may have to be more flexible on your dates. Regularly check sites like SecretFlying and The Flight Deal for deals and specials you might not catch on your own. For example, a few days before I wrote this, Secret Flying announced that they had found a round-trip fare from Philadelphia to Orlando for $106 on American Airlines. When you see one of these fare alerts, you'll need to jump on it, because chances are it won't last long. Of course, it will be easiest to take advantage of deals like these if you live in or near a large city or hub airport. If you're less flexible with times, you can use price-watching websites and apps like Hopper, SkyScanner, Airfare Watchdog, Smarter Travel, FareCompare, KAYAK, Orbitz, and Expedia that will alert you when it's the best time to book. Keep in mind that extreme budget airlines such as Spirit and JetBlue charge extra for every little thing to make up the money they have lost on those cheap tickets. Research and plan ahead so you don't have to pay extra charges you weren't expecting.

If you're planning to rent a car upon arrival, you may want to look at alternative airports to Orlando International Airport. Orlando-Sanford International Airport is on the north end of the Orlando metropolitan area, approximately 50 miles from Walt Disney World. If you choose this airport, you might want to time your arrival and departure so you aren't navigating Interstate 4 traffic through downtown Orlando during rush hour. Other airports within driving distance are Tampa International Airport (77 miles) and Daytona Beach International Airport (74 miles).

Will you be parking your vehicle at the airport, and if so, how much will that cost over the time you're gone? Then when you arrive in Orlando, will you want to rent a car? Many hotels, and especially Disney-owned properties, provide a free airport shuttle and transportation to the parks. If you want to go to a grocery store or pharmacy during your stay, or want to do something outside the Disney resort area, you might prefer the freedom of a rental car. You can also do rental car price comparisons on sites like Orbitz, Kayak, and Expedia and add these to your spreadsheet. Consider the size of car you'd require, the need for additions such as car seats or navigation, and the cost of added taxes or insurance. Don't be afraid to do a search for smaller, local, independent companies that might offer better rates; just check reviews before renting. Look for discounts through AAA (American Automobile Association) and CAA (Canadian Automobile Association), through your auto insurance provider, and through warehouse club stores like Costco if you're a member. Also weigh whether it would be worth it to use a service like Uber or a taxi service instead of renting a car if you need to go anywhere. Of course, keep in mind that most ride-share services don't have car seats for children. A compromise would be pricing out a shuttle for the trip from the airport; then if you know you'll need a run to the grocery store, planning to have one adult take an Uber or taxi to the store and back while the other adult stays with the children. If you plan to rent a car, check with your own car insurance or credit cards to see if they provide coverage of your rental before you purchase additional insurance from the rental car company.

To contrast with your flight expenses, you'll want to add up what it would be to drive your own vehicle to Disney. Open a map service like Google maps and put in directions from your house to zip code 32836 (the zip code for part of the Walt Disney World resort) in order to get a rough idea of how long it would take to drive there. Is it a reasonable distance? Remember that the timeline given by Google maps does not include stops. You'll want to add a couple of hours for meals, bathroom breaks, and gas station stops. Speaking of gas stations, how much does it cost to fill your vehicle with a tank of gas? How many tanks of gas will you need for a round-trip drive to and from Disney? Add those to your spreadsheet. Will your trip require one or more overnights? Where would those be, and how much would they cost? Consider breaking up the trips with stops at friends' and relatives' houses along the way to save hotel costs (and reconnect with people!) Add hotel costs to your spreadsheet as well, and don't forget to factor in meals you'll need along the road. How about tolls? Keep in mind there are several toll roads in and around Orlando, including the Florida Turnpike if you will be driving south from I-75. You can calculate tolls on the Sunpass site.

Armed with this information, you should be able to compare the cost of flying vs. driving. Usually one or the other will make more financial sense; but if you're still torn, ask yourself a few more questions. Do I want to take my family through the hassle of airport security, limit our luggage, and worry about missed and delayed flights and lost bags? Is it worth the time spent in the car to save money by driving instead of flying? Is my car safe, comfortable, and reliable enough for a long road trip? Do I want to spend my vacation time driving instead of having more time at my destination? How important is it to me to have the freedom of driving my own car and setting my own timetable? Will the kids drive me nuts if we are stuck in the car together for that long?

If you are thinking about driving but don't want to spend the money on gas and wear-and-tear on your vehicle, check AutoDriveaway and see if there are any opportunities for transporting someone else's vehicle to and from your destination.

What kind of hotel do we want to stay at?

Your choice here basically comes down to on-property or off-property. How important is it that you stay at a Disney resort on Disney property? It's a pretty good bet to assume that a Disney resort hotel will be more expensive than an off-property hotel. However, that isn't always the case! Disney has some very affordable hotel options. And if you and your family enjoy camping, that can be an even better value, and can even be done right there on Disney property!

Staying on-site at Disney

Disney offers six basic categories of places to stay, broken out by cost. Here is a table showing average cost per night at writing time, for one night in the summer. Disney excludes taxes and fees when it presents these estimates.

Table 1: Disney resort categories, before taxes

Category	Average cost	Pros and Cons	Resort Names

Deluxe Villas	$330-545	larger rooms, sleeping more people; more "home-like"	Saratoga Springs, Old Key West, Polynesian Villas, Bay Lake Tower at Contemporary, Villas at Grand Floridian, Animal Kingdom Villas, Boardwalk Villas, Beach Club Villas, Wilderness Lodge Villas
Deluxe Resort Hotels	$289-569	Disney "themes"; good restaurants on-site; usually convenient to parks	Animal Kingdom Lodge, Polynesian Village, Grand Floridian, Wilderness Lodge, Beach Club, Contemporary, Yacht Club, BoardWalk
Moderate Resort Hotels	$166-309	Themed resorts; require a longer bus or boat ride to parks	Caribbean Beach, Port Orleans, Coronado Springs, Fort Wilderness Cabins
Value Resort Hotels	$93-124	Bright and colorful; small rooms; thin walls; limited dining on-site	Pop Century, All-Star Music, All-Star Movies, All-Star Sports, Art of Animation

Campgrounds	$52	Rate is for a tent or pop-up camper.	The Campsites at Fort Wilderness Resort
Other Select Deluxe Hotels	$157-250 depending on room	Run by Sheraton & Westin; dining on-site; convenient to Epcot; convention traffic	Dolphin, Swan

Why stay at a Disney property?

You may be wondering what advantages you would gain by staying on Disney property at one of their resorts vs. staying off-property at a chain or independent hotel. There are several advantages that make them worth your consideration.

1. Extra Magic Hours – Every day, one or two of the theme parks open early or stay open later, usually one extra hour (but can be up to three), exclusively for Disney resort hotel guests. This is your chance to experience the parks when they are a little less crowded, and encounter shorter wait times for rides.
2. Early access to FastPass+ reservations – Disney resort hotel guests can book FastPass+ reservations, which is like jumping ahead of the line, for three attractions or shows per day 60 days in advance of your visit. Guests who are not staying at a Disney resort can only reserve FastPass+ reservations 30 days in advance!

3. Free transportation and parking – This is one of those money-saving tips to consider once you're on your vacation. If you're bringing your own car, it costs $20 per day to park at one of the theme parks! Even some non-Disney hotels, like Shades of Green, charge for parking. Disney resorts also offer the Disney's Magical Express bus service to and from the airport, with luggage transfer, for free. If you are flying and decide to stay off-site, you'll want to factor in the cost of an airport shuttle, or see if your hotel offers airport shuttle service, in order to do an accurate cost comparison. Disney also advertises that their transportation is free for Disney resort guests, but in reality it's free for anybody on Disney property once you're there; you don't have to be staying at a Disney resort to ride the buses, boats, and monorail.

4. Disney Dining Plans – Here is another potential money-saver! Staying at a Disney resort offers access to one of the Disney dining plans. We'll look at these plans in more detail later, but it's definitely something to consider, especially if you plan to spend all your time on Disney property. A Disney Dining Plan will also help you keep tight control of your food budget. They won't be the best choice for everyone, though.

5. Convenience – If you're not planning to venture outside the Walt Disney World resort, staying on Disney property at a Disney resort is best place to be. All the resorts have easy access to the Disney theme parks, attractions, and other resorts via bus, boat, and monorail.

6. The full Disney experience – Many people find that staying on-site at a Disney resort hotel provides that extra touch of "magic" that makes their vacation

complete. Most resorts have whimsical theming that may reflect Disney characters or movies, ensuring the theme park experience doesn't stay at the theme park. For those with small children, this is an especially effective way to bring their Disney experience to life through the entire vacation.

If you decide you do want to stay at a Disney resort hotel, the next step is to look for deals! Consider the time of year you want to visit. Large crowds usually mean fewer discounts. Think about the times school is normally in session – those are the less crowded times when rooms are likely to be cheaper. If you are limited to the summer months, spring break, or holidays like Christmas and Thanksgiving, things can get more expensive. Sticking to the less costly resorts can help keep prices down year-round, though.

Picture 1: The monorail seen from the grounds of the Polynesian Village Resort

Staying off-site

Your other choice is staying at a non-Disney hotel. Your options here are almost unlimited. There are hotels and resorts for every budget around Disney. You can also look at non-traditional options such as vacation home rental, condominium rental, bed and breakfast, and even AirBnB (a quick search there showed individual rooms-for-rent starting at $70 per night – and if you're just looking for a place to crash, it's something to consider!)

If you are going with a larger group of people, like extended family or friends, splitting the cost of a vacation home can be an economical option. This is also a good option for a large family. A Google search reveals hundreds of possibilities, from property management companies to vacation rental by owner. Most of the vacation homes in the Walt Disney World area are clustered to the southwest of the Disney World complex, so you will need to have access to a car, but these homes can be surprisingly affordable – as little as $50 per night (although the average will be between $100-200), many with private pools. The cost can go down quite considerably if you are splitting it with others! Be aware that most vacation homes have a minimum stay requirement. Another cost-saving benefit of a vacation home is its kitchen, which will allow you to prepare some meals there and save a considerable amount on dining!

Then there are the usual hotel options, including every chain you can think of and some independent hotels you didn't know about. There will be rooms for every budget and price range; be sure to look for amenities such as airport and theme park shuttle buses to make them comparable to Disney resorts. If you are a collector of frequent traveler points for certain hotel chains, this is the time to figure out whether you have enough points to offset the cost of your stay, or whether you can use a rewards credit card and other strategies to gain the points you need before you book. We'll look at some of these tactics a little later.

Food is another reason to stay off-site; choosing a hotel that offers a free breakfast will definitely save you some cash. Many off-site hotels are located near multiple restaurant options that will not only keep you from feeling like you're stuck paying Disney prices for Disney restaurants, but also allow you and your kids to have familiar food options you're used to having at home.

There are multiple resources you can check to find a place to stay in the price range you want. Sites like Kayak, Expedia, Travelocity, Tripadvisor, and Hotels.com offer search engines that allow you to narrow down your options by area, price range, and star rating (quality). Trivago is a metasearch site that checks all these other sites to find the lowest price for each hotel. If you want to stay at a particular hotel, you can always check the website for that hotel or chain and see if they are offering any specials. Once you've narrowed down a hotel and are ready to book, it won't hurt to call the front desk or the hotel's 1-800 number and see if they can offer you an even better deal than what you've found online.

Sites like Priceline and Hotwire allow you to bid for hotels in your price range, area, and star level if you aren't set on a particular hotel or chain. A great resource to check if you decide to go this route is the website BetterBidding.com – it offers terrific guidelines for bidding, including lists of which hotels you may end up reserving and what winning bids have been submitted for these hotels. Be aware, though, that if you decide to get your hotel through a bidding site, there are no refunds and no cancellations – you're completely stuck with whatever you get.

If you and your family enjoy camping, that's another option that may decrease the cost of your stay at Disney. There's an Orlando/Kissimmee KOA that offers tent sites, RV spots, and even cabins. They even list specials on their website. A Google search will bring them up along with several other nearby campgrounds. Tent spots start at less than $50 a day.

If you want to take a risk to get a really good deal, you can download the Hotel Tonight app. This app searches local hotels for unfilled rooms to find you a great deal. The downside is that you could find yourself hopping from place to place in search of a bargain.

Timeshare Presentations

Another way to travel for less is to sit through a timeshare presentation (without the intention of buying) in exchange for vacation freebies and discounts. In order to do this, you need to be willing to give up *at least* three hours of your vacation to sit through the presentation, and have the willpower to be able to say no to every single tactic they throw at you. Many people love their timeshares, but if you are reading this book because you are struggling to afford a Disney vacation to begin with, investing in a timeshare is probably not the best financial decision you could make!

Timeshare companies are always looking for leads, but if you're looking at booking a Disney vacation and don't have anyone calling you to offer one, your best bet will be to go to the websites for the major timeshare companies such as Hilton Grand Vacations, Marriott Vacation Club, Starwood Vacation Network, Diamond International, etc. and signing up to receive more information. A Google search for timeshares in Orlando will also net you a list of places to start. Once the company contacts you, ask if they have any current promotions so you can see exactly what you would be getting into. You can even check eBay and Craigslist for timeshare promotions. The ads often look personal but are actually placed by salespeople looking to generate leads. Look for keywords like "presentation." Make sure to find out if the "special" price they are advertising is for the entire stay or one night.

You'll also need to ensure you meet the company's requirements to take their "free" vacation or package. Otherwise you may end up owing the cost of the trip. Make sure to read terms and conditions very carefully! Be aware if you have children that the presentation often requires both spouses to be present.

Then, all you need to do is enjoy your vacation, but also sit through the timeshare presentation. Be prepared for a hard sell, multiple agents, several hours of your time, and different sales tactics to get you to buy. The salespeople will try to overcome all your objections. Stand firm, and you can get a greatly-discounted vacation. I have not done this myself, but I know others who have and are happy with their vacation experience and savings. I've also heard from people who question the ethics of accepting vacation discounts and benefits from a company, and taking up the time of the salespeople, with no intention of buying. In the end it will be up to you to decide your feelings about this strategy.

Please note that Disney Vacation Club does not offer free vacations for attending their presentations. We will talk about them a little later, but they simply don't operate like a traditional timeshare company, which includes not offering freebies and discounts.

Military Discounts

One more option for members of the armed services is the Shades of Green resort. Formerly known as the Disney Inn and Disney Golf Resort, this hotel is now run as an Armed Forces Recreation Center. Shades of Green is worth mentioning for both its location and its price. It is literally across the street, within walking distance, from the Polynesian Village Resort and its monorail stop. Shades also has its own shuttle service between the resort and the theme parks and attractions, and Shades guests are eligible for Extra Magic Hours just like Disney resort guests! There is even an on-site AAFES store where you can buy souvenirs and sundries without paying tax. The pools have been recently remodeled, and the grounds are beautiful. If you plan on playing golf during your stay, it's the most convenient location possible.

Who is eligible to stay at Shades of Green? First, the people you would expect: active or retired U.S. military, National Guard, Reserves, or 100% disabled service members; surviving spouses; and foreign military while assigned or attached to a U.S. military unit or installation. In addition, though, current and retired Department of Defense Civilians and family members, uniformed Public Health Service and NOAA members, and other categories are also eligible. Please see the eligibility page on their website to check if you are eligible. When you check in, you'll need to be prepared to show your military ID and a current leave-and-earnings statement.

Veteran, but not currently serving or retired? Every January and September, Shades opens up their eligibility to all veterans; you simply need your DD-214 to book.

My family is eligible to stay at Shades of Green and we do so every chance we get. We love its convenience and pricing. It's a short walk to the Polynesian to ride the monorail and visit other resorts and the theme parks. Negative reviews note that it costs $5 per day for parking, the on-site restaurants are marginal, and the hotel and rooms are impersonal for a Disney-themed hotel. If you are looking for Disney "magic" in your hotel room, this may not be what you want.

Prices at Shades of Green range from $98 a night to $400 for a suite and are categorized on a sliding scale depending on rank; they also offer discounts and specials at various times of the year. See the Shades of Green website for more details.

If you are military but really want to stay on-site at a Disney resort hotel, it's also possible to do that at a discount. Disney offers Armed Forces Salute rooms at prices up to 40% off. You'll have to call the Disney reservation line to get the details on these offers as they vary depending on resort and time of year; there are sometimes blackout dates, and resorts to which the discount will not apply. Alternatively, you can visit the Information, Tickets, & Travel office at your local base and they will be able to give you all the details and help you find the best deal.

Picture 2: The grounds at Shades of Green Resort

Florida Resident Discounts

Florida Resident Discounts aren't just for theme park tickets. They can also get you valuable discounts on Disney hotels and resorts. Disney has their own Florida resident discount page – it's focused on theme park tickets, but there is a link under "Resort Reservations" that says "Find out more." If you click this link, it brings you to a dedicated special offer page for Florida Resident Discounts. At time of writing, they were offering up to 25% off room rates on Disney resorts. If you aren't a Florida resident but will be traveling with friends who are, see if they could book your room for you at the same time that they're booking yours, and you can pay them back. (They'll need to be the ones to check in, with Florida ID, to receive the discount.)

Chapter 4: Budgeting for Park Tickets

The next step for creating your Disney budget will be factoring in park tickets. There's no way around it; getting into the theme parks requires a ticket, which requires payment. Disney offers so many ticket options it can be overwhelming, and prices change frequently. There are deals to be had, though, if you know where to look.

Gate Prices

If you were to go up to the gate and buy your Disney tickets, these would be the prices you'd encounter as of writing this article. (All the prices below were obtained from a travel agent, not on the Disney website – please see the Disney website for the most up-to-date pricing information.) As you can see, Disney likes to charge a little extra for a single-day ticket to the Magic Kingdom since it's their signature park, and the most in-demand. Multiple day tickets do not include an extra charge for the Magic Kingdom.

If you have a child who will be age two or under at the time of your trip, you're in luck, because that child does not need to pay for a ticket. (And yes, it is possible to take a baby or toddler to the theme parks and have a great time; I've done it myself!) For ticket purposes, Disney classifies an adult as age 10 and up, and a child as ages 3-9. Please note that prices vary depending on attendance date; Disney increases prices when they expect large crowds, like during holidays or school vacations.

Table 2: One park per day prices at the gate – before tax

1 Day Adult – Epcot, Hollywood Studios, Animal Kingdom	$121.41
1 Day Child – Epcot, Hollywood Studios, Animal Kingdom	$115.02
1 Day Adult – Magic Kingdom only	$132.06
1 Day Child – Magic Kingdom only	$125.67
2 Day Adult	$215.13
2 Day Child	$202.35
3 Day Adult	$308.85
3 Day Child	$289.68
4 Day Adult	$346.13
4 Day Child	$324.83

You also have a choice between limiting each day to only visiting one park, or buying a more expensive ticket that will allow you the flexibility of "hopping" from park to park. These are called parkhopper tickets. Which ticket you decide on will depend on your budget and the priorities you set for your trip. I've presented the prices for parkhopper tickets in a separate table for clarity.

1 Day Adult	$174.66
1 Day Child	$168.27
2 Day Adult	$273.71
2 Day Child	$260.93
3 Day Adult	$367.43
3 Day Child	$348.26
4 Day Adult	$419.61
4 Day Child	$398.31

As you can imagine, this is where most people get discouraged. If you were to take your family of two adults and two children for four days and wanted the parkhopper option, tickets alone would cost you an eye-popping $1,635.84! That's an expensive vacation considering you still need to budget for food and drinks, souvenirs, hotel, and transportation!

Don't despair, though. There are ways to figure out how to pay less than the gate price for park tickets.

Military Discounts

If you or your spouse is a member of the armed forces, Disney offers some substantial deals to show their support for the military. To be eligible, the purchaser must be a member of active or retired US & foreign military, National Guard, active Reserves, or 100% disabled. Note that these tickets are not available to separated (non-retired) veterans, or family members of the military member purchasing tickets without the military member present.

The best deal for military tickets is the "Disney Salutes the Armed Forces" pass. Disney renews offering these tickets every year, and there is always the chance that they will not offer them the next year. From time of purchase, you have within the same year to use them – in other words, whether you buy your ticket in January, June, or December, the pass will expire December 31. There are three varieties of Armed Forces Salute tickets, and they are the same price regardless of whether you are purchasing for an adult or a child.

Table 4: Disney Salutes the Armed Forces ticket prices

4 Day Parkhopper	$194.50
4 Day One Park + 4 "Fun and More" Tickets	$194.50
4 Day Parkhopper + 4 "Fun and More" Tickets	$228.00

The "Fun and More" option includes tickets to DisneyQuest, water parks Typhoon Lagoon and Blizzard Beach, Disney miniature golf courses, and a few other attractions.

To purchase Armed Forces Salute tickets, you'll need to go through the Information, Tickets & Travel office on your local base, go through the ticket office located at Shades of Green resort, or purchase them at the gate at Disney World by showing your military ID.

Florida Residents

If you are a Florida resident, you're in luck! Disney offers discounted tickets to Florida residents. The bad news is that not every type of ticket is discounted, and that there are blackout dates for these specially-priced tickets.

Table 5: Florida Resident ticket prices — before tax

3 Day Adult One-Park-Per-Day Ticket	$185.50
3 Day Child One-Park-Per-Day Ticket	$172.80
4 Day Adult One-Park-Per-Day Ticket	$205.30
4 Day Child One-Park-Per-Day Ticket	$191.50
1 Day Adult Parkhopper Ticket	$128.00
1 Day Child Parkhopper Ticket	$122.00
3 Day Adult Parkhopper Ticket	$210.00
3 Day Child Parkhopper Ticket	$197.30
4 Day Adult Parkhopper Ticket	$236.50

4 Day Child Parkhopper Ticket	$222.80

Blackout dates for these tickets are usually the entire summer from the beginning of June through the beginning of August; the last two weeks in December; and most of April. Basically, anytime school is not in session. They also have an expiration date of December of the year in which you buy them, and they will also expire 6 months from the date of first use. Proof of Florida residence must be presented at purchase and use these tickets. Unfortunately, it isn't possible to buy and/or use Florida resident tickets as a non-Florida resident. IDs are checked at the gate, and it won't work! Timeshares don't count as residences in Florida, either.

Discount Tickets

So you're not in the military and you don't live in Florida – now what? Now's the time to look for other sources of discount tickets.

Consider the time of year you plan to visit. Disney does not keep their ticket prices the same year-round; they vary them depending on season. On the Disney website, you can find a calendar that will tell you the dates when their tickets are less expensive. It may not be a huge difference, but it's something. The other benefit is that during these "off-season" times of year when Disney prices are lower, hotels tend to lower their prices as well. The parks are also likely to be less crowded. If you have school-age children, you will have to decide whether or not they should miss school to take a Disney vacation in the off-season, since school holidays tend to coincide with higher prices.

If you know where to look, there are several well-known, reputable discount ticket brokers in the business. They buy tickets wholesale from Disney and re-sell them at a slight mark-up. Savings on Disney tickets can add up to between $3 and $40 off gate prices. That may not sound like a huge amount, but when you add up the number of tickets your family will require over a number of days, it can be a substantial discount. Some of the best-known brokers are Undercover Tourist, Getaway Today, ParkSavers, and Maple Leaf Tickets. Other discount ticket brokers also offer this service, but may not be as reputable. I don't recommend getting tickets from Craigslist or from eBay or other auction sites, because no matter how persuasive the listing, you have no way of knowing whether or not the tickets are really genuine, unused, or have days remaining on them.

Some AAA (American Automobile Association) and CAA (Canadian Automobile Association) offices offer discounts on Disney tickets to their members. Check with your local office to see if they do.

Timeshare companies also offer inexpensive Disney tickets in exchange for spending a couple of hours at their hard-sell presentation. If you do a Google search for discounted Disney tickets and see sites advertising $35 tickets, or billboards along the interstates leading to Disney World, they are probably selling timeshares. See the section on timeshare presentations in the previous chapter for more information about what's involved.

Picture 3: Seven Dwarfs Mine Train at Magic Kingdom

Should I Get an Annual Pass?

This question may seem surprising if you don't live within an easy distance of Disney, but it's actually worth some thought, depending on the length of your stay. The main reason is for the benefits that come with the pass. Only one person in your party has to have a pass to receive the benefits. The cost of one adult four-park annual pass is $749.00 before tax (current price with tax is $797.69), but that also gets you free parking at the theme parks (a $20 value per day), unlimited PhotoPass downloads (a $149 value), and a 10% discount on most food and merchandise purchases. Room discounts can be up to 30%, although they vary. You also get a fun newsletter every month, and the sheer pleasure of being able to say you hold an annual pass!

So, if your family of two adults and two children is planning a trip to Disney and considering an annual pass for one of the adults, here is the break-even point minus all those extras:

Table 6: Cost of 2 adult and 2 children's parkhopper tickets vs. 1 adult annual pass + 1 adult and 2 children's parkhopper tickets

Number of Days	1	2	3	4	4+1	4+2	4+3
4 parkhopper tickets	$685.86	$1,069.28	$1,431.38	$1,635.84	$2,321.7	$2,705.12	$3,067.22
3 parkhopper tickets and 1 annual pass	$1,308.89	$1,593.26	$1,861.64	$2,013.92	$2,525.12	$2,809.49	$3,077.87

As you can see, the cost of purchasing one annual pass and all the other tickets as parkhoppers will almost break even if you are buying tickets for seven or more days at the theme parks, and it goes down from there. If you include all those other benefits, though, it may be worth thinking about before you reach that point. For example, if you were to take a car and park at the theme parks every day of your visit, you'd start saving money with an annual pass at the six-day point since parking alone would cost $100 over those days.

There are additional annual pass options if you want to add water parks and other extras. If you are a Florida resident, the cost of an annual pass is not only lower, but can be paid in monthly installments without interest.

Other Theme Parks

If you still think tickets to Disney World are too expensive for you, you have other options. Consider Universal Studios, Sea World, Busch Gardens, and Legoland. There are several other attractions in the Orlando area to allow for a fun and fulfilling vacation without ever setting foot on Disney property. For the sake of argument, let's compare the gate cost of three-day tickets to each of these attractions for a family of four.

Table 7: Gate prices for other theme parks – without tax

Disney World	3 day parkhopper tickets for 2 adults and 2 children	$1,431.38

Universal Studios	3 day park-to-park (Universal Studios and Islands of Adventure) tickets for 2 adults and 2 children	$899.96
Sea World	Unlimited admission through December 2016 for 2 adults and 2 children	$396
Busch Gardens	Unlimited admission through December 2016 for 2 adults and 2 children	$556
Legoland Florida	Unlimited admission through December 2016 (including water park) tickets for 2 adults and 2 children	$396

Note that Sea World and Busch Gardens only offer either single-day tickets or unlimited admission through the end of the year, the equivalent of an annual pass, which is why we've listed the price of an annual pass. Sea World and Busch Gardens also offer combination tickets with each other, and Sea World offers combination tickets with Universal Studios. For Legoland Florida, tickets jump from two-day to annual pass, so we've listed the price of annual passes.

Sounds better, right? It's important to keep in mind that Busch Gardens is in Tampa and Legoland is in Winter Haven, both a few hours from Orlando (Legoland is closer). You also might run out of things to see in three days at these other parks, although there are definitely three days' worth of attractions at Universal Studios. A combination of Disney tickets and tickets to these other theme parks might be the most economical way to go for you and your family, combining Disney magic with a slightly cheaper – but still fun – alternative. Keep in mind that if you are staying at a Disney resort you will need to have your own transportation to these other theme parks, and you will not be able to use the Disney Dining Plan there. See the next chapter for information on Disney Dining Plans.

Other Disney Options

Consider saving a day of theme park ticket fare by doing something else on Disney property. Disney has two water parks, Typhoon Lagoon and Blizzard Beach, and a miniature golf course, Fantasia Mini Golf. There's also the Disney Springs shopping and dining complex (formerly Downtown Disney). Housed at Disney Springs is Disney Quest, a virtual entertainment attraction which is kind of like a more sophisticated arcade. You could also consider taking a day to explore the Disney resorts with their unique theming, or just see what's at your hotel or resort and spend some time at the pool. Your family may appreciate the downtime.

Budget for Souvenirs

Instead of breaking this out into a separate chapter, I'll just include this subject in the ticket section since souvenirs are part of the theme park experience. Don't forget that there are gift shops on every corner of the World and in every hotel and resort. Every member of your family will want to take home some special memento of their trip. Your budget for these could vary from very tight to extremely large, depending on what you're thinking of purchasing. We'll give you some tips for keeping this line item reasonable in a later chapter, but for now just don't overlook allocating some money in your budget for souvenirs.

Chapter 5: Budgeting for Food at Disney

Food is one of those expenses that can vary wildly. You can bring loaves of bread and jars of peanut butter for each person and live on that your entire trip, thus rendering your food budget almost zero, or you can dine in fancy table-service restaurants for every meal, ordering appetizers, entrees, desserts, and cocktails, bringing your food budget to astronomical levels. Of course, for most people the reality will be somewhere in between. It's hard to estimate a food budget when you don't know how much you'll spend, but estimating it is a good idea so you won't be taken by surprise when you're on your trip. Plus, if there are any particular restaurants at which you are determined to eat, you'll want to make Advanced Dining Reservations (ADRs) as far in advance as possible to secure a table.

First, have a look at the variety of restaurants available at Disney. Go to the Disney website and browse the selection. Are there any that stand out to you as a must-visit? Disney now offers menus for each restaurant online so you can get an idea of the selection and the price range. Estimate how much the meal will cost you and your family. What would you order? Would you add extras like drinks other than tap water, and desserts? Don't forget to factor in a tip. That should give you a good idea of how much you can expect to pay for a Disney dining experience.

Now, in your spreadsheet you should be able to calculate the cost of breakfast, lunch, and dinner for each of the days of your trip based on that estimate. Don't forget to add some extra for snacks. There will be temptations all over the parks, and you'll want to be able to allow for some of those. Add up your food expenses – is there anywhere you can cut back?

If you're determined to keep your food budget down, either limit the number of table-service restaurants you plan to dine at, or eliminate them all together. Check various websites for Disney restaurant reviews so that you aren't disappointed by spending a large amount of money for mediocre food. Consider eating breakfast in the room; muffins, instant oatmeal, cereal bars and yogurt (if your room has a fridge) are good, quick, cheap choices, especially when you want to spend more time getting started with exploring the parks than you do sitting down to eat a meal. There is an entire section in the chapter on saving money while on your vacation dedicated to saving money on food.

Disney Dining Plans

If you're staying at a Disney resort hotel, you'll be able to enroll in a Disney dining plan. What's that? It's a way to pre-pay for all your meals and snacks while you're at Disney World. Of course, the next logical question is: is it worth it? As usual, the answer will be: it depends.

In order to qualify for a Disney dining plan, you will need to sign up for Magic Your Way tickets. This is basically a way to purchase your hotel, park tickets, and dining in one big package. A travel agent can help you do this, or you can do it yourself on the Disney website. The Disney dining plan is like a voucher system; you're allotted a certain number of meals and snacks per day during your trip. There are three "levels" of dining plan, each priced for adults (ages 10 and up) or children (ages 3-9).

Quick-Service Plan	2 quick-service meals 2 snacks	$46.34 adult/$20.18 child
Dining Plan	1 quick-service meal 1 table-service meal 2 snacks	$67.33 adult/$24.22 child
Deluxe Dining Plan	3 meals and 2 snacks per person (does not differentiate between quick-service and table-service meals)	$103.57 adult/$37.62 child

There are two additional levels of add-ons to the Deluxe Plan, the Premium and Platinum plans. These include the same dining options as the Deluxe Plan, but the Premium and Platinum Plans also include several recreational activities (golf, fishing, etc.) and the Platinum Plan includes spa treatments at some of the resort spas. For purposes of comparison, we won't include these two plans since their "extras" do not involve dining.

In order to figure out whether these are a good deal for you and your family, you need to understand what's included and what's not included. A quick-service location is pretty much any of the fast-food style, counter-service restaurants at the parks and resorts. For breakfast, lunch, and dinner, a quick-service meal includes an entrée and non-alcoholic beverage. (In the 2016 plans, a quick-service meal included one dessert, but that has been eliminated in the 2017 plans.)

What is a snack? Figuring that out can be a little trickier. A snack can be anything from a single-serve box of popcorn (if it isn't in a souvenir container), to an ice-cream bar, to a coffee or soda.

Please note that alcoholic drinks are never included as part of the dining plan. Gratuities are also not included except at dinner shows, room service for resorts that offer it, and at Cinderella's Royal Table. Children are required to order from the children's menu, which could be an issue if your kids have big appetites or are adventurous eaters who want to try new foods. That's why the children's prices for the Dining Plans are so much cheaper than the adult prices.

All the dining plans also include a refillable drink mug per person. You can use this mug at any of the self-service beverage stations at the quick-service restaurants in the resorts (not the theme parks). If your family drinks a lot of soda, this might be something to consider!

Table-service restaurants are basically any restaurants in which you are seated by a host or hostess and waited on by a server. They also include some dinner shows and character dining, but you may be required to use more than one dining credit on those events. Table service credits include one dessert per day in the 2017 plan.

Now the big question: is it worth it?

Let's compare one day on the plan vs. one day not on the plan for a family of four, two adults and two children, visiting the Magic Kingdom and see who comes out ahead. We're going to assume our family uses one credit per person at each establishment (i.e., doesn't go to special dining experiences that require additional credits that day.)

First, the Quick-Service plan, which is the least expensive. Our fictional family of four has paid $133.04 for their dining plan for that day (2 adults at $46.34 each, plus 2 children at $20.18 each.)

Table 9: Quick-Service Dining Plan comparison

Breakfast	1 snack per person	Main Street Bakery and Café: 1 Strawberry Smoothie $4.49 1 Banana Chocolate Chip Coffee Cake $3.29 1 Cinnamon Swirl Coffee Cake $3.29 1 Classic Coffee Cake $3.29
Lunch	1 quick-service meal – includes entrée and non-alcoholic drink.	Be Our Guest Restaurant: 1 Braised Pork $16.99 1 Croque Monsieur $13.99 1 Kids' Carved Turkey Sandwich $8.49 1 Kids' Whole-Grain Macaroni $6.99 4 Fountain beverages at $3.29 each = $13.16

Dinner	1 quick-service meal– includes entrée and non-alcoholic drink.	Cosmic Ray's Starlight Café: 1 Barbecued Pork Bacon Cheeseburger $14.99 1 Bacon Deluxe Chicken Sandwich $11.99 1 Kids' Chicken Breast Nuggets $6.99 1 Kids' Turkey Sandwich $6.49 3 Bottled Water at $3.00 each = $9.00 1 Milk $1.99
Snack	1 snack per person	Snack Cart: 4 Mickey Ice Creams at $3.75 each = $15.00
Total	$133.04 Value	$140.43 to buy separately

As you can see, our family saved $7.39 by using the Disney Quick-Service Plan. Of course, for this exercise I just chose random menu items, not necessarily the most expensive item on each menu. If you were to carefully choose to maximize your dining plan value by choosing the most expensive item on the menu at each restaurant, it's more likely you'll save a lot more money using a dining plan. And if you are only buying the cheapest items on the menu, you might be wasting money by using a dining plan.

You'll also notice that using one snack credit per person for breakfast means that you'll either have to drink the free water with breakfast, purchase drinks separately, or use another snack credit for your breakfast beverages. Since you can vary your Dining Plan credits day-to-day, you might choose to do this and forego those Mickey ice cream bars one of the days on your trip.

Now let's look at the regular Dining Plan. We'll once again assume we are looking at a family of two adults and two children visiting the Magic Kingdom and using one credit per meal. For this plan, our family of four has paid $183.10 for that day (2 adults at $67.33 each, plus 2 children at $24.22 each.) For simplicity, let's pretend our family has purchased the same breakfast (using their snack credits), lunch, and snack as they would have selected using the Quick-Service plan. That only changes their dinner to a table-service restaurant.

Table 10: Dining Plan comparison

Breakfast	1 snack per person	Main Street Bakery and Café: 1 Strawberry Smoothie $4.49 1 Banana Chocolate Chip Coffee Cake $3.29 1 Cinnamon Swirl Coffee Cake $3.29 1 Classic Coffee Cake $3.29

Lunch	1 quick-service meal – includes entrée and non-alcoholic drink.	Be Our Guest Restaurant: 1 Braised Pork $16.99 1 Croque Monsieur $13.99 1 Kids' Carved Turkey Sandwich $8.49 1 Kids' Whole-Grain Macaroni $6.99 4 Fountain beverages at $3.29 each = $13.16
Dinner	1 table-service meal– includes entrée, non-alcoholic drink, and dessert.	Tony's Town Square Restaurant: 1 Spaghetti $21.00 1 Caesar Salad with Chicken $18.00 1 Kids' Cheese Pizza $10.00 1 Kids' Spaghetti $11.00 2 Bottled Water at $3.00 each = $6.00 1 Tiramisu $8.00 1 Gelato $7.00 (Kids' meals include a choice of beverage and dessert – tricky!)

Snack	1 snack per person	Snack Cart: 4 Mickey Ice Creams at $3.75 each = $15.00
Total	$183.10 Value	$169.98 to buy separately

In this case, our family did not save money using the dining plan vs. purchasing the food options on their own. The dining plan also does not include a tip, which you would want to leave at the table-service restaurant. (That would be an additional $13.20 based on 15% of the individual prices for our imaginary dinner.)

Finally, let's compare the most expensive dining plan, the Deluxe Dining Plan. Our family paid $282.38 per day for this plan (2 adults at $103.57 each, plus 2 kids at $37.92 each). Here, we've added quick-service breakfast at Be Our Guest and changed lunch to a table-service meal. We've kept dinner and snacks the same as they were on the previous dining plan example.

Table 11: Deluxe Dining Plan comparison

Breakfast	1 quick-service meal – includes entrée and non-alcoholic drink.	Be Our Guest: 1 Feast a la Gaston $24.00 1 Croissant Doughnut $24.00 2 Coffee at $2.49 each = $4.98 1 Kids' French Toast $14.00 1 Kids' Scrambled Eggs $14.00 2 Milk at $1.99 each = $3.98

Lunch	1 table-service meal – includes appetizer, entrée, non-alcoholic drink, and dessert.	Liberty Tree Tavern Restaurant: 1 Sweet Corn Fritters $7.00 1 New England Clam Chowder $8.50 1 Tavern-Battered Fish and Chips $18.00 1 Pilgrims' Feast $19.00 1 Ooey Gooey Toffee Cake $7.50 1 Boston Cream Pie $8.50 1 Kids' Chicken Noodle Soup $2.50 1 Kids' Apple Slices $2.50 1 Kids' New England Pot Roast $11.00 1 Kids' Macaroni and Cheese $9.50 2 Soft Drinks at $2.99 each = $5.98 (Kids' meals include a choice of beverage and dessert)

Dinner	1 table-service meal– includes appetizer, entrée, non-alcoholic drink, and dessert.	Tony's Town Square Restaurant:
		1 Zucchini Fries $11.00
		1 Calamari $15.00
		1 Spaghetti $21.00
		1 Caesar Salad with Chicken $18.00
		1 Kids' Cheese Pizza $10.00
		1 Kids' Spaghetti $11.00
		2 Bottled Water at $3.00 each = $6.00
		1 Tiramisu $8.00
		1 Gelato $7.00
		(Kids' meals include a choice of beverage and dessert – tricky!)

Snacks	2 snacks per person	Main Street Bakery and Café: 1 Strawberry Smoothie $4.49 1 Banana Chocolate Chip Coffee Cake $3.29 1 Cinnamon Swirl Coffee Cake $3.29 1 Classic Coffee Cake $3.29 Snack Cart: 4 Mickey Ice Creams at $3.75 each = $15.00
Total	$282.39 Value	$321.30 to buy separately

This time, our family has saved quite a lot of money by using the dining plan. An obvious reason is the very expensive breakfast at Be Our Guest. But it also looks like they spent an awful lot of time sitting and eating, and ordering an awful lot of food. A good question to ask yourself is: if you were paying for all this without using a dining plan, would you really be buying all of that?

Character dining experiences and dinner shows are usually the most expensive meals at Walt Disney World, so if they're a "must-do" for you, you'll want to do the math on the dining plan and see if it would be worthwhile. You are most likely to save money by using some dining credits on these otherwise-pricey meals.

The other question to ask yourself is: do you really want to spend the time on one or more sit-down meals every day of your trip? Most table-service restaurants require advance dining reservations, which lock you into a time; this can be inconvenient if you find yourself on the other side of the park from your restaurant when it's nearing your reservation time. Sit-down meals also take time. Disney is used to turning tables over fairly rapidly, but you can still expect to spend about an hour at each sit-down meal.

Of course, your choice of meals and restaurants will also influence whether or not you will save money by using the dining plan. After all, do you really want to pay $21 for one plate of spaghetti? At that kind of pricing, you'll want to choose your restaurants carefully, especially if you do not purchase the dining plan. Some quick-service restaurants are absolutely delightful, and some table-service restaurants are no better (or sometimes worse) than what you'll find at any American chain. This is where it pays to do research before your trip and carefully narrow down the restaurants you want to choose.

You also don't have to use your dining credits evenly. For example, if you only want to use one snack credit one day and three another day, you have the flexibility to do that. Some people report using remaining snack credits to purchase candy and other packaged food items to bring home as souvenirs and gifts at the end of the trip!

Occasionally, Disney will offer "free Dining" as part of a booking package. What you need to know is that they will either throw in the dining plan or discount rooms, but not both. So before you jump on a "free dining" special offer, consider whether it's more worthwhile to you to get a room discount instead.

Picture 4: the Canada pavilion at Epcot

Figuring Out your Food Budget

Now that we've had a look at the Disney Dining Plans and some typical menu prices, you'll have a better idea of what you want to spend on food. Make sure to budget enough to cover each day of your trip. If you do decide to purchase a Disney Dining Plan through a Magic Your Way package, remember that you'll be paying for all of it in advance – this could actually be helpful when you are trying to spread out the costs of your trip instead of facing a large bill when you are on your way home from vacation.

If you aren't staying at a Disney resort, you won't be eligible for one of the Dining Plans anyway. In that case, or if you've decided the Dining Plans are not for you, you'll need to think of a rough estimate for how much you want to spend per meal, and put that in your spreadsheet. Will you be going to a grocery store at the beginning of your trip, and cooking and eating in your hotel for any meals? Remember, you can even eat muffins, fruit, instant oatmeal, and coffee in a hotel room without a kitchen if you are looking to save time and money before hitting the parks every morning. We'll discuss some other money-saving strategies for your trip food budget in a later chapter of the book.

Chapter 6: Trim the Fat from your Household Budget

Okay, you've established a household budget and a Disney trip budget. Now what? Now is the time to try to bring them together by really sitting down and studying that household budget. Have the rest of your family join you. This part of your plan to afford Disney will require real buy-in from everyone involved. You may even want to talk to your children about the new spending plan, and let them know that you might have to say "no" to some things and have slightly leaner birthday and/or Christmas celebrations in the near future because you're trying to get the money together to take a family trip to Disney World. I think you will be surprised at how readily your kids will understand and agree to a leaner spending plan when they have this goal in mind! They may even have a few fundraising ideas of their own.

In order to reach your savings goal, you'll want to keep careful track of those savings. It's no good cutting coupons or trimming your budget only to "lose" that savings amount by not tracking the difference. There are several ways you can do this: a small notebook, a computer spreadsheet, or a phone app. The important thing is to write down every penny saved and move those pennies into your Disney vacation fund.

Your Disney Vacation Fund

There are a couple of ways to hold onto your needed Disney fund. Disney offers their own vacation accounts now, and there is always the old-fashioned method of starting a savings account solely for your trip. If you go this method, you can check Bankrate.com for current interest rates and find the highest interest rate for savings accounts, or you could do a search to find current offers and incentives for opening bank accounts. If you are a member of a credit union, check to see if they have a "vacation club"-type account where you can deposit money solely for this purpose.

The Disney Vacation Account is a relatively new way offered by Disney itself to allow customers to pay for their vacations. With a $10 minimum initial contribution, U.S. residents can start their own account. Disney has also included their own (rather vague) budget-estimating tool and contribution-estimating tool, to help you set and reach your goal. You can use the Disney Vacation Account to save for up to five years before your vacation, using automatic or anytime contributions. The obvious downsides to this method are the failure to earn interest on your savings and the restriction of these funds to a Disney vacation only. The benefit is that when you use your account to purchase your vacation, you will receive a $20 Disney gift card for each $1000 spent. Basically, it's like you've earned 2% interest on your money. That's pretty good, but shop around before you decide to start one, and make sure you're okay with the restrictions on using the account. It does offer tools for keeping track, and you can deposit money in any increment.

Picture 5: Fourth of July fireworks over Magic Kingdom, seen from World Drive

Cost-Cutting Strategies

In studying your budget, you'll want to look for places you can "trim the fat." What spending can you cut to afford your trip to Disney? Here are some places you can frequently cut costs to save money.

Cable – are you still paying for cable television? Do you really use it that often? If you're using your Netflix, Amazon Prime, Hulu, or similar streaming accounts more than television cable, it may be time to cut the cord. Hooked on sports? There are still ways to watch live sports events without cable. For about $20 a month, you can sign up for Sling TV, which will allow you to stream ESPN and several other channels. It's not subscription-based, so you can quit paying as soon as football season is over. Some sports associations offer their own streaming video channels, or a simple online search for "how to stream live sports" will come up with some websites and YouTube tutorials; the sites change too often for me to list any here. If you still think you can't live without cable, call your cable provider and tell them you're thinking of cutting it because it's too expensive. See what kind of deal they offer you.

Cleaning – don't hire someone to clean if you can do it yourself. Use vinegar and baking soda to clean almost every surface instead of buying expensive cleaning supplies. Use less dishwasher soap and laundry detergent than the instructions call for; modern appliances clean so efficiently that less is needed, and the instructions could be calling for more than you need so that you'll buy the product more often. Look into making your own laundry detergent for just pennies per load. Check Pinterest for ideas.

Clothing – downsize your clothing budget. Shop at thrift stores and consignment stores. Treat low-priced stores like Ross, T.J. Maxx, and Marshall's like a treasure hunt. Use consignment stores to sell back clothing you've stopped wearing or doesn't fit before you purchase anything new. Choose items that don't need dry-cleaning to save that expense.

Don't try to keep up with the Joneses – ignore or mute ads on television and radio. Toss catalogs into the recycle bin without even opening them. Before they reach your inbox, set your e-mail to auto-delete messages from your favorite stores letting you know they're having a sale so you aren't tempted to go window shopping for things you don't need. Remember that social media should not be a competition; don't let yourself get jealous about your neighbors' things. Think of the payments they are making instead. For every purchase, ask yourself if the item is a need or a want. Sleep on it.

Electricity – try turning your thermostat up just one degree in hot weather or down just one degree in cold weather. You may find that the difference is not noticeable but results in a savings on your bill (compare to the same month last year). Pester your family to turn off lights, appliances, and faucets when they aren't in use, or invest in timer switches. LED light bulbs are cheaper than ever, and according to the Department of Energy can save you 75% or more on your electric bill. If it's too big an expense to switch out all your light bulbs at once, just do one a month, or change them as the old ones burn out. Another advantage of LEDs is their long lifespan, which means you will save money by going years without having to replace them. If LEDs are still too expensive, you can also save by switching to CFL bulbs – they just won't save you quite as much as LEDs in the long run. The Department of Energy has a helpful website about the different types of bulbs available.

Entertainment – are you really getting a good value out of your streaming video services? Consider cutting those to a cheaper plan, or cutting them out altogether. If you frequently go to the movies, think about waiting for those movies to come out on DVD or streaming services instead, and renting them to watch in your home. Use free streaming music services like Pandora or Spotify instead of paying for a subscription to satellite radio. Invite friends over for drinks rather than going out for happy hour or nights out on the town. Swap babysitting services with another family so that each of you can enjoy a date night with free child care. Do date nights at home after the kids are in bed. Get a library card and take advantage of your local library's selection rather than buying new books, or become a frequent customer of your local used bookstore; resolve to sell back a book each time you buy a new one. Rent video games rather than purchasing them, or buy them used. Become tourists of the free attractions in your area rather than spending money; check out local parks, museums, and picnic spots.

Gas – use an app like Waze or GasBuddy to compare the pump prices at gas stations near you.

Gifts – give homemade gifts. Buy gifts throughout the year based on what's a good deal rather than waiting until the holiday season. See if friends and extended family will agree to stop exchanging gifts with you, or if you have a large extended family and everyone is used to buying gifts for everyone else, float the idea of drawing names in a gift exchange. It's possible they could be relieved at the idea of saving money as well. See if you and your spouse will agree to not exchange gifts, or require the other person to come up with something creative that doesn't cost anything, and put the money you've saved into your Disney fund. Check Pinterest for ideas.

Grooming – learn to cut your family's hair, especially children's. There are countless helpful tutorials on YouTube and other online sites, and the cost of haircutting supplies will pay for themselves after a few trims. You may even decide to cut your own hair, if you just need a trim across the bottom. If you color your hair at a salon, consider finding a great color at the drugstore and coloring your hair at home. Practice giving yourself pedicures and beauty treatments. Find a beauty training school and get a professional treatment for much less. Try switching to drugstore makeup and beauty products rather than more expensive options.

Gym – do you really use your gym membership? Are you getting a good value out of it? Can you explore the idea of exercising at home, or walking, jogging, or biking through the neighborhood instead? Ask a friend or neighbor to join you to increase your accountability. Check streaming video services like Netflix and Amazon Prime for exercise videos, check them out from the library, or check charity shops for donated DVDs and equipment. Check with your workplace to see if they provide wellness incentives or gym membership discounts or reimbursements.

Health care – if you need prescription glasses, ask your optometrist's office for your prescription and purchase your frames online. You could save a large amount that way. For recurring prescription medications, see if it's cheaper to receive them by mail. Also, shop around for prescriptions – not every pharmacy charges the same copay for the same prescription. Compare prices at pharmacies in chain and independent drugstores, grocery and discount stores, wholesale clubs, and reliable online pharmacies like HealthWarehouse that operate within the US and display the Verified Internet Pharmacy Practice Site symbol ("VIPPS"). Check GoodRx to learn the fair price of your medication. Especially if you are paying cash, don't be afraid to ask for a discount. Check and see whether a generic version of your medication is available, and if it would be cheaper to purchase it out-of-pocket than with insurance. Also see if you can save money by getting a 90-day prescription instead of one that will last a shorter length of time.

If you are eligible, look into signing up for a health savings account. This will allow you to pay a regular fixed amount tax-free to a fund that will roll over from year to year. Then when you have medical expenses, you can get reimbursed from that fund, saving you taxes. A flexible spending account is another way to accomplish the same result, but does not roll over from year to year.

Holidays – buy decorations just after the holidays when they are deeply discounted and put them away for the next year. Buy gifts throughout the year as you see good deals – but keep a record so you don't forget what you already bought people. Make homemade wrapping paper out of newspaper, paper bags, or children's drawings. Save and reuse gift bags. Make homemade decorations for your home. Check Pinterest for ideas.

Household goods – consider investing in an Amazon Prime membership. I buy so many everyday items on Amazon, from diapers to cat food, and use their Subscribe & Save feature to save even more. Amazon Prime also gets you two-day shipping on a number of items (although be sure to compare the costs of all sellers of an item so you aren't paying more with Prime) and includes entertainment through their streaming video service. If it's still cost-prohibitive, you can actually share a Prime account with another person using Amazon Households – then you can ask that person to pay you back for their half of the cost of membership with you when you sign up. Just be aware that even if you aren't living in the same house, you have to share payment wallets with the other member. That means they have access to your credit cards and could in theory use them to make Amazon purchases, so it should be someone you trust.

It's a good idea to download the Amazon app and comparison shop when you're in a store. You may find the same item that you were about to buy is cheaper on Amazon. Prices on Amazon are dynamic and change frequently, so another good resource is a site called Camel Camel Camel that tracks the prices on Amazon of the items in your wish lists, and alerts you when something is a good deal.

Walmart and Target are also trying to get a piece of the Amazon pie. Walmart has started a similar service called ShippingPass, which gets you free 2-day shipping on any item from Walmart.com for about half the cost of Amazon Prime. Target has started a Subscribe and Save program, plus with the Target REDcard you receive 5% off all purchases and free shipping on any order. The nice thing about the REDcard is that there is a debit card option so you don't have to open a new credit card account if you are worried about racking up credit debt.

Try Jet for a low-price alternative to Amazon.

Don't forget to look for items on eBay, Craigslist, thrift and charity stores, local Facebook groups, garage and yard sales, and even Freecycle before paying full price.

Household Maintenance – do your own lawn care and house cleaning. Paint your own walls. Investigate doing your own lawn treatments and pest control. Learn basic home repairs so you don't have to hire someone to fix something that breaks. Think about whether you really need to replace something that's broken, or whether it can be repaired for less. For car repairs, use a site like Repair Pal to compare estimates of repair prices near you.

Insurance – shop around for better insurance rates than you're paying at least once a year, especially for car insurance. The companies that advertise themselves as "cheaper" aren't always the least expensive for every situation, and rates change all the time. Some companies give discounts for holding several forms of insurance with them at once, such as car, homeowners' or renters' insurance, and life insurance.

Online purchases - don't even think about making a purchase before you check for coupons at sites like RetailMeNot! There are all kinds of other online sites where you can check for coupons and discount codes before checking out. Shop through a points-earning site like Swagbucks, Ebates, or ShopYourWay to maximize your savings. Download the Paribus app, which scours your email and Amazon orders to find out what you've bought recently that has decreased in price, then pays you that difference without you having to lift a finger. The Paribus app keeps 25% of that difference, but if you use my referral link to sign up they will only keep 20%, allowing you to put 5% more back in your pocket: https://paribus.co/i/D4Jmlr When you sign up, you'll get your own referral link, and for every person you sign up the company will lessen their take by 5%.

Samples – want to get stuff for free? Check what's available on CoolFreebieLinks.

Software – before you purchase software, check online to see if there is a free version that has all the features you need. We talked at the beginning of the book about OpenOffice and LibreOffice, but there are also free versions of other frequently-used software applications. Instead of purchasing Photoshop, for example, try the Editor at Pixlr to professionally edit images. Check reviews at CNET to find free versions of other software applications you need. Downloading software from unknown sources can be dangerous, however, so regularly back up your data and make sure you have a good virus-scan program on your computer to guard against malware.

Telephone – do you really need a land line? If you already have a cell phone, consider cutting the phone cord and saving that monthly bill. I also know people who won't give up their land lines because they don't get very good reception on their cell phones. In that case, look into switching either to the cheapest mobile plan possible, or even moving to a no-contract phone in case of emergencies. If you have a smartphone but don't like to use it to call people, consider giving up your cell contract for it and only using it on Wi-Fi. It's not difficult anymore to find free Wi-Fi all around the country. Even if you only have a cell phone, look into switching to a cheaper plan. Are you using all the minutes or all the data you're paying for? Would you save money with a different provider? If you don't want to purchase more data but would come close or exceed your data limit every month, the free app Onavo Extend claims to extend your plan by compressing your data, thus saving you money. How about using an app like Skype to call people instead of your phone's minutes?

If you want a land line and also plan to keep cable, see if your cable company is offering deals on bundling cable with a cable telephone line.

Transportation – look into car or vanpools to save money on gas and wear and tear on your vehicle, or if possible, consider biking, walking, or taking public transportation. If you are making a substantial car payment or paying for premium fuel, consider downsizing. If you have to pay for private transportation somewhere, consider using Uber or Lyft instead of a taxi service.

Don't neglect performing regular maintenance on your car. Check tire pressure and fluid levels regularly. Keeping your vehicle in good shape will prevent costly repairs down the road.

Water – cut down on your water usage and encourage your family to do the same. It will not only save you money, it's good for the environment. Turn off the faucet when you're brushing your teeth. If you have a low-flow shower head, it probably uses less water to take a shower than a bath. If it's legal in your area, build a DIY rain barrel to collect water for your garden – you can collect hundreds of gallons of water in one every year. A search for "how to build a rain barrel" will bring up multiple tutorials and instructions.

Most importantly, keep careful track of every penny saved and mark it down. Then transfer that amount to your Disney fund.

Save on Your Grocery Bill

There are many easy ways to save on your monthly grocery budget.

- Quit eating out – this one is obvious. Most Americans have stopped cooking at home[1]. And yet, eating at restaurants and ordering take-out will add up to a big chunk of your food budget. Cooking at home is a chore, but it can save you substantially in the long run, and that's all money that can go to your Disney fund. Let's compare the cost of making a homemade pizza vs. ordering one from a pizza delivery chain.

---

[1] "The slow death of the home-cooked meal," The Washington Post, March 5, 2015 https://www.washingtonpost.com/news/wonk/wp/2015/03/05/the-slow-death-of-the-home-cooked-meal/

Table 12: Cost of making vs. delivery pizza (prices sourced at Publix in August 2016 and Pizza Hut in July 2016)

Pizza at home	Pizza delivery
2 packages fresh deli pizza dough: $6.58	Large 1-topping pepperoni pizza: $11.99
1 jar name-brand pizza sauce: $4.95	Large pizza with olives, mushrooms, green pepper, onions, and pepperoni: $19.99
1 16-oz. bag name-brand shredded mozzarella cheese: $6.79	Delivery fee and tip: $7.92
1 package name-brand pepperoni: $3.99	
Small can sliced olives: $1.49	
1 pint sliced mushrooms: $2.00	
1 green bell pepper: $1.27	
1 red onion: $1.71	
Total Cost: $28.78	Total Cost: $39.90

As you can see, if you were to make instead of order pizza once a week, you would save $578.24 over the course of a year! That doesn't even take into account the possibility of spreading out the ingredients over more than one meal, or using less expensive store-brand ingredients rather than name-brand. And the bonus is that children LOVE helping make homemade pizza. Give it a try! And if you *would have* gone out for pizza otherwise, keep track of those savings and add them to your Disney fund. If you don't want to bother making your own pizza at home, buying a frozen pizza will still be cheaper than delivery.

That's just one example. If you have a favorite restaurant dish, try to recreate it at home. Get out your crock pot and use it more often – with the bonus of having dinner ready at the end of a long day. Make breakfast for dinner. Get the kids involved in cooking and give them a task of choosing and preparing a meal for the family once a week. Look at thrift stores for cheap household appliances that could make cooking fun, like Panini presses, indoor grills, and fryers. Try new recipes.

- Plan your meals – it's so important to have a plan so that you don't end up with take-out or restaurant meals on impulse. Do you have a favorite grocery store? Carefully study the weekly ad for that store and plan meals around the items that are on sale. It can become a fun challenge to try to plan as many meals using as many sale items as possible in a week. Then, stick to your plan! Post it prominently so that everyone knows what's for dinner every week and there are no surprises. Make sure to thaw meat in time for cooking so you aren't caught in the "Whoops, I forgot to thaw the chicken, let's just order a pizza" trap, and think of backup meals that can be made from pantry ingredients on short notice (like fishcakes made with canned salmon and breadcrumbs, or spaghetti). Plan crock pot and freezer meals to save time and money – if you're making something that freezes well, make a double batch and freeze half for another meal. Or just make an extra portion of that evening's meal to take to lunch the next day. Save money on meat by eating more vegetarian dishes.

Try a meal rotation schedule. If your family doesn't need a lot of variety, make a regular schedule of meals and serve those every week. For example:

Sunday: Breakfast-for-dinner

Monday: Hot dog night

Tuesday: Crock pot soup or stew

Wednesday: Spaghetti

Thursday: Grilled cheese sandwiches

Friday: Stir fry with some kind of meat, leftover vegetables, and rice or noodles

Saturday: Homemade pizza

- Search for budget meals – Pinterest is a great site to find all kinds of budget meal ideas. A simple online search can also net you plenty of blogs and sites that will help you plan inexpensive meals at home. The U.S. Department of Agriculture also has a website about eating healthy on a budget.
- Save money at work - bring lunch and snacks to work instead of buying them. If you have leftovers from dinner, don't be squeamish about taking those to lunch the next day. Never buy from the vending machines; keep a stash of snacks at your desk instead, having bought them in advance at the grocery store or discount store, where they're cheaper. Bring in a thermos of coffee every day instead of buying coffee at work or on the way to work. If you like fancy flavored coffee, get some flavored syrups and learn to make the equivalent of your favorite beverage at home. Even cutting back on purchased coffee to a few days or once a week will save you a bundle over time.

- Clip coupons – you don't need to take up extreme couponing as a hobby in order to save money with coupons. The key is to keep track of each coupon's savings amount and deposit that money into your Disney fund. Study the weekly ad for your favorite grocery and discount stores so that you can try to match coupons with items as they come on sale. Check grocery store websites and apps for digital coupons if you don't have time to clip. There are dedicated websites for most stores that can aid you in maximizing your savings, such as TotallyTarget, IHeartKroger, WildForCVS, etc. Do a search for how to save money at your favorite store, and you'll probably come up with a helpful site. These sites will also give you great tips for collecting and using coupons. One overall site that can help you save money specifically for a Disney trip is Couponing to Disney. Here you will encounter likeminded individuals who are exploring innovative ways to fund their Disney vacations.

  Remember, you don't have to buy a newspaper to get access to coupons these days. You can go to sites like Coupons.com for large numbers of printable coupons on name-brand products. Increase your earnings by printing them through a site like Swagbucks that gets you points there every time you use a coupon. Do a search for stores near you that will double or triple coupons!

  If you find high-value coupons you won't use, try selling them individually or in lots on eBay. There is a thriving market for coupons there.

- Price compare at stores – check the grocery store ads, either online or in the newspaper, and see what similar items are priced. If you have to buy certain items name-brand, comparison shop at a few different stores and see who carries those items at the least expensive price. Just make sure you aren't spending more in gas or tolls to shop at more than one store in your enthusiasm to get a deal. Keep a notebook or use an app to keep track of different prices at different stores. You may be surprised to learn that a store that you thought had the lowest prices really doesn't. Apps like Flipp can help you compare sale prices at local stores.

- Price compare items by unit – supermarkets are experts at making you think you're getting a good deal when you really aren't. Don't just look at the large price under the item; read the fine print to find the price per unit, such as ounces. You can use unit prices to compare the costs of fresh, frozen, and canned foods, and from brand to brand, to make sure you are getting the best deal.

- Shop seasonal – Shop baking goods and spices around the holidays when they are on special. Look for lunch items around back-to-school time, and stock up if they're non-perishable. Study when produce is in season and buy large amounts at that time; can or freeze what you don't use for later in the year. Buy turkeys or turkey breasts after Thanksgiving and Christmas when they are on sale. Freeze them and use them throughout the year. You can use one bird for several evenings' worth of meals.

- Take shortcuts – buy powdered milk for cooking and baking. You won't be able to tell the difference when you're not drinking it straight. Grow fresh herbs instead of buying them; basil and parsley are especially easy to grow. Compare ingredients in name brands and store brands; you'll often find the store brands are much less expensive while offering the same ingredients as the name-brand item.

- Don't shop hungry – this is a well-known tip. When you're hungry, you're more likely to buy impulse items you don't need. Make a list, shop on a full stomach, and stick to that list.

- Look outside eye level – grocery stores put their most enticing, highest-priced items at eye level, in hopes that you'll grab them when they catch your eye. Look above and below that level to see if you can find a similar product to one you are trying to find at a better price.

- Don't waste food – according to the U.S. Department of Agriculture, food waste costs a family of four an average of $1,500 per year[2]. Don't waste food! Only buy what you will use. Have a plan for each and every fruit and vegetable you buy, and stick to that plan. Buying in bulk can be a great cost-saver for dry goods, but if you won't eat that entire bag of apples before they start going bad, you aren't getting a good deal. Plan a leftover night every week or have a plan to turn leftovers into a new meal – like making chicken soup out of a rotisserie chicken and the odds and ends of vegetables in the produce drawer. Learn to can and preserve foods so you can enjoy today's fresh, seasonal produce later as jams, jellies, relishes, and salsas (these also make inexpensive yet highly appreciated homemade gifts). If certain fruits and vegetables are in season now, they're worth canning, preserving, and freezing for those months when they will be more

---

[2] "Let's Talk Trash," U.S. Department of Agriculture, ChooseMyPlate.gov, 2 September 2016, https://www.choosemyplate.gov/lets-talk-trash

expensive. Take the time to clean out and reorganize your fridge, freezer, and pantry so food doesn't get forgotten in the bins or the back. Remember that the "best by" or "sell by" dates don't necessarily mean that an item has gone bad. (Pay attention to "expires on" dates, though, to ensure safety, and trust your senses of smell and taste.) Research what items freeze well and what don't – some surprising foods can be frozen, like milk and bread. Don't be shy about taking items that spoiled too soon back to the store for a refund. I recently took back a pint of strawberries that molded the day after I bought them; the store refunded my money with no questions asked.

The U.S. Department of Agriculture has a helpful website that gives tips and ideas on how not to waste food.

- Spend a little to save a lot – there are plenty of services out there ready to help you save on your grocery bill. The subscription website Emeals will send you a weekly menu plan and grocery list based on the sale items at your local grocery store. If you stick to their plan, it's easy to budget and save money every week. You can do this yourself by studying the ads and making your own meal plan, but a service like Emeals can save you time. I know a family who uses a meal-ingredient delivery service as a budgeting tool. With both adults working full-time, they used to buy take-out and go to restaurants much more often than they should have because it was just easier than planning meals and doing frequent shopping. Plus, they are foodies, so they enjoy gourmet meals. The service sends all the ingredients and recipes for three gourmet meals a week – all they have to do is the prep, cooking, and cleanup. It costs $60 per week for the three-meal plan, but that family is actually saving money and eating healthier. This may not work for everyone, especially if you are a savvy shopper and a careful meal-planner, but it works for them.

- Use apps – apps like iBotta, ReceiptHog, Checkout51, Shopmium, MobiSave, SavingStar, Ebates, Shopkick, NCP, and other sites give you cash back for scanning your receipts after you go grocery shopping. These sites usually incentivize certain items by acting like a coupon – if you can show an item on your receipt, you can get a certain amount of cash back on it. SavingStar links your store loyalty cards to get cash back as well. Apps like GroceryIQ can help you meal plan and make a grocery list to help you stick to your budget.

- Check receipts for surveys – on those occasions you do order pizza or eat in a restaurant, see if the receipt contains a link to a survey you can use to rate your experience in order to get something for free or a percentage off your bill on your next visit.

- Use paper coupons when eating out – also check your mail and sites like Groupon, Retailmenot, SnipSnap, CouponSherpa, and the websites of restaurants themselves for coupons and specials if you do plan to eat out or order pizza. Sign up for your favorite restaurant's e-mail list to try to get discounts.

- Join the club – if you will get your money's worth out of a warehouse club membership, they can be a great place to save money, especially on items like diapers, paper goods, and medications. Do the math first to ensure that whatever savings you are obtaining in comparison to regular supermarkets and discount stores add up to more than the annual membership fee.

Also be certain that you would use the store often enough to make it worthwhile; I had a membership in a warehouse club for a while, but it was so far out of my way that I ended up going so rarely that I lost money. Check online blogs to find out which items are the best deals at the store to which you are a member. Don't buy bulk amounts of food if they'll spoil before you can use them up; that's false economy.

If you don't want to join a warehouse club but want to pay similar prices, check out Boxed. Since they operate online, they don't need to charge membership fees to offer similar pricing to the warehouse stores. Enter code OFKHJ at checkout for a discount. They also offer free shipping over a certain amount, free shipping on your first purchase after you sign up, and frequently post additional discount codes on their site. They also have an app for convenient shopping on your phone or tablet.

- Beware the dollar store – it may seem like a great idea to buy some of your groceries at stores where "everything is a dollar" or "everything's $5 and under." Things are not always as they seem, though, and sometimes a name-brand item that looks like a great deal because it's so much cheaper than you'd pay at another store is actually in a much smaller package. Or, the price per unit is much higher because there is less of the item than in the package you'd buy at a regular grocery store.[3]

---

[3] "How big food brands are boosting profits by targeting the poor." The Washington Post, February 7, 2015 https://www.washingtonpost.com/news/wonk/wp/2015/02/07/how-big-food-brands-are-boosting-profits-by-targeting-the-poor/

- Pay with cash – if you withdraw a cash amount to cover your weekly grocery shopping and force yourself to stick to that amount, it can really make you think about what items you want versus what items you need before you toss things into your cart. Many people use a system of cash envelopes to stick to a budget; the Mvelopes app is an electronic way to do the same thing. Make it a game to try to stay under your budget – anything you don't spend that week gets deposited into your Disney fund!
- Grow your own – for a relatively small investment, you can start a garden that will produce a bountiful harvest of fruits and vegetables for your table. Tomatoes, cucumbers, zucchini, and fresh herbs can be easy to grow and turn into a fun hobby.

There are so many ways to save money on your household budget. You can find numerous other books and sources of information to help you trim your expenses. But just cutting spending isn't the only way to fund a Disney trip – you can also try to make a little more money. We'll explore how in the next chapter.

Chapter 7: Increasing Your Income

You may think you are maxed out for earning potential, but there are always ways to earn a little extra. Some of these are almost painless and take very little time and effort. Maximizing what you put into them, of course, will increase what you get out of them.

Sell Your Stuff

Look around. What do you have sitting around your house and garage that you don't need or use? What's just taking up space and creating clutter? Could any of that stuff be sold for a profit? As a recent bestselling book suggested, look at each item and ask yourself if it brings you joy; if not, sell it.

- Books – check with local used bookstores to see if they buy back books. Become an Amazon seller and sell your books there. You can even sell used books at auction sites like eBay. To maximize your profit, plug in each book's ISBN number at BookScouter or DirectTextbook and you can find out which online sites will net you the most money in cash or gift cards for your books. BookScouter even has an app that allows you to scan the book to find out its value. This works especially well for textbooks! Some people even go to sites like eBay and scour the used textbook auctions for books they can purchase for less than they can get for them, using BookScouter to determine their profit margin. If you do this enough it could add up to hundreds of dollars a month.

- Board game pieces – Do you have board games sitting around that are missing pieces? Ever come across games in the thrift store that don't have all their pieces? Take those loose parts and sell them on eBay. There is a thriving market for individual game pieces or bags of multiples.

- Clothes – if you have clothes in good condition that you don't wear anymore taking up space in your closet, don't donate them. Sell them! Local consignment stores will pay you when your items sell. There are also chain consignment stores like Plato's Closet and Once Upon a Child. Check sites like eBay, Poshmark, BuffaloExchange, ClothesMentor, CashInMyBag, and ThredUp for online versions of the same service. Look for enormous once- or twice-yearly consignment sales at which you can sell your clothes with a built-in audience of shoppers. Think long and hard about whether you really want to keep maternity clothes and baby and children's clothes. If you suddenly need these again, you can always buy a fresh wardrobe from the same places you've sold your old clothes to!

- Music, Movies, and Video Games – eBay and Amazon are the first places to consider when selling these items. SecondSpin and Decluttr are other sites that buy used DVDs, CDs, and games. You can also sell used video games at Gamestop, Best Buy, and other video game retailers. Also check out Target's trade-in program, which also buys back game systems and other devices; they don't accept every game or device, but they do tend to give good prices for the ones they take.

- Cell phones – upgraded your cell phone recently? You can probably get decent money for your old one. eBay, SellCell, Amazon, Gazelle, and even retailers like Walmart and Best Buy all buy used cell phones. Always make sure to wipe your data before you sell your phone! And if none of these sites are offering very much for your phone or you don't want to go to the trouble of selling it, you can use it for making money at home – we'll show you how in the next section.
- Laptops – the site Cash Your Laptop not only buys laptops, but also phones and tablets.
- Jewelry, coins, and collectables – do you have any old jewelry you don't wear anymore? A coin or similar collection you never look at? You could think about selling it. Find a jewelry store or coin collection store and get an appraisal. They may even offer to buy it from you. Pawn shops are another option, but you will most likely get the best price from a private buyer on eBay. Coins aren't the only collectable currency – make a note of your bills' serial numbers and check them against the list of unusual, collectable serial numbers at Cool Serial Numbers.
- Junk mail – yes, you can even sell your junk mail! Sign up for SBK Center and they will give you points for paper junk mail and email. Those points can be exchanged for Visa gift cards.
- Anything else – there's always the old-fashioned garage or yard sale to purge your stuff. Throw one yourself or get together with neighbors to increase traffic and share the workload. If you don't want to devote most of a weekend to a purge, you can sell items one at a time on sites like eBay and Craigslist. There are also new, dedicated sites with apps like LetGo and

OfferUpNow. Most areas, even small towns and rural areas, also have online "garage sale" Facebook groups where you can sell your stuff to interested locals. I have seen many things for sale on these sites that I would not have previously thought would be worth the effort of posting, like extremely used clothing, shoes, broken toys, and even open packages of diapers! There is a buyer out there for almost any item in almost any condition, and selling on a Facebook group that isn't open to everyone, where you can see people's profile pictures and locations, is a safer way to do business than to sell on a site like Craigslist. If you do sell on Craigslist, try to meet your buyer in a public place, especially if you are selling an expensive item.

An alternative to selling your things is to loan them out. Loanables allows you to rent out just about anything to people local to you, including clothing, tools, games, sporting equipment, and even cars and boats. If you have a lot of designer clothing in good shape, you might consider lending it out on Style Lend.

Earn Gift Cards for Online Activity

There are multiple online sites that will enable you to earn gift cards by performing simple tasks like watching videos, filling out surveys, or shopping through their links. Over a two-year period, I used just two of these sites (Swagbucks and Perk) to earn over $1,400 in gift cards – and that was with very minimal effort. It's possible to approach these earning methods like they're your job and earn much, much more than that. Since I buy a large number of items on Amazon, I cash the points I earn at these sites in for Amazon gift cards. This offsets my general household spending budget, and if it's money I would have spent anyway I can put the equivalent amount in my Disney fund. Other people use their points to buy Disney gift cards in a roundabout way since they aren't offered at these sites. They'll get gift cards for stores like Target, and then use those cards at those stores to pay for Disney gift cards. There's more information later about Disney gift cards. I've heard of people paying for their entire Disney vacations using points from these sites.

- Earn Swagbucks - Swagbucks is one of the best-known sites for earning gift cards. It has several methods for earning points (which are called Swagbucks, of course), including watching videos on your phone or desktop PC, answering surveys, playing games, searching through their search engine, and shopping through affiliate links. There are several apps you can download to earn Swagbucks. The two I use most frequently are EntertainNow and SBTV. After playing each video on these apps, you earn Swagbucks. In SBTV, the shortest videos are usually the "10 Second Tips" under the Home & Garden category. If you do an online search, you can find out which videos on all the other apps are the shortest. Then you can save those videos to your list of Favorites on the app, and every day just go play the videos in your Favorites. This allows you to earn Swagbucks much faster! The video apps max out after a certain number of videos are watched, so you have to either switch between their different apps every day or use their other methods to make Swagbucks. If you qualify for surveys, that's an easy way to earn points as well. Once you earn a certain number of Swagbucks, you can cash them in for gift cards. (I always cash in in $25 increments.) If you want to sign up for Swagbucks, don't do so without checking for a signup code to get you bonus Swagbucks on sign-up. The Couponing for Disney site has their own signup code to get you more Swagbucks than you would get signing up for it on your own. You can also earn Swagbucks by getting other people to sign up. So if you find you enjoy earning Swagbucks as an easy way to earn gift cards, let your friends and family know, and ask them to use your affiliate link when they sign up. And if you've found this book to be helpful, please sign up with my referral link: http://www.swagbucks.com/refer/mmb10863

- Start a Perk farm – Perk is another site where it's easy to earn gift cards from online activity. The quickest, easiest way to earn Perk points is through playing videos on your phone, although you can also earn them through searches, playing games, and answering surveys. Download the PerkTV app, select "Movie Trailers," and pick the first one in the list – it will continue to play automatically from there. The beauty of Perk is that you can set the videos to playing on your devices, and then basically leave them alone. Every few hours they will pop up a message that says, "Are you still watching?" which you have to acknowledge to continue. You can play videos on up to five devices at the same time on the same Perk account. This is a great thing to do with those discarded phones sitting in a drawer after you've upgraded them; you just have to make sure they are up-to-date enough to run the app and play the videos without getting hung up. As you build up gift cards with Perk, you can decide to purchase inexpensive Android phones in order to create a "Perk farm" and maximize your point-earning potential. Good phones for running Perk can be found for $20 or less if you know where to look (and on Black Friday, I bought four phones for $5 each from Best Buy online; Dollar General is another good place to look on big sale dates). If you and your spouse each have a Perk account, you can earn an average of $1 a day per device – enabling you to earn a few gift cards a week! Once again, if you've found this book helpful, please use my referral link to sign up: http://perk.fm/4uiyn

Picture 6: The author's Perk farm

- Microsoft Rewards – if you default your search engine to Bing instead of Google, you can also earn reward points for gift cards. Plus, you get to see a new pretty picture on their home page every day! You can earn up to 15 points per day by doing searches on your PC (that's two searches per point) and 10 for searching on your phone. Bing also highlights some daily offers to allow you to earn extra points, such as clicking a link to a video or answering some trivia questions. Remember that you don't have to think up 50 new search terms on a daily basis. Use Bing to go to websites you would normally just type in the address for. Then, if at the end of the day you still haven't maximized your points, you can put in something random like "cupcake recipes" and Bing will pop up a list on the side or bottom of the page of "Related searches." You can click one of those items, then click something on the list of related searches that pop up for that search, and on and on until you've earned all your points for the day. Since this doesn't require any thinking, it can take just a few seconds to earn all your points. 500 points (or 475 once you've reached Gold status after a certain number of searches) is all it takes to earn a $5 gift card, and it's amazing how quickly you can get there just through simple internet searches. Details can be found at Bing when you sign up for an account.

- Install an app – if you don't have privacy concerns, install the Smart Panel app. They will pay you to collect data from your phone on what websites you use and how much time you're spending online. Get $5 for qualifying and $5 for every month you keep the app installed.

Another app that tracks your online activity in exchange for cash and gift cards is MobileXpression. They have a version for both iPhone and Android. There is also the SlideJoy app. Instead of tracking your online activity, it pays you to put an ad on your lock screen. It's currently only available for Android, but the company plans to offer an iOS version in the future.

- Watch TV – if you watch a lot of TV, you can log on to Reward TV to answer trivia questions about the shows you watch. It's a Nielsen company, so you are assured that they are legitimate. They give you cash and gift cards for your trivia answers.

- Other sites – these are not the only sites out there for earning gift cards, if that's your goal. Others you may want to investigate include Viggle and MyPoints and survey sites like Vip Voice, I-Say, and SurveySpot. Using the Amazon Trade-In Program can net you gift cards for your old stuff. Sites and apps like iBotta, ReceiptHog, Checkout51, Shopmium, MobiSave, SavingStar, Ebates, Shopkick, and NCP offer online coupons and incentivize receipt-scanning with cash back and gift cards.

Keep in mind that if you earn a certain number of gift cards through these sites in a given year, you will have to fill out a W-9 and the sites have to submit a Form 1099 for taxes. I'm not a tax expert, so look for details on each website's terms and conditions.

Become a Salesperson

We all know that one friend (or several!) on social media who is selling a product. Whether you like the product they are selling or not, the reason they are doing it is because it works! Not every time – no doubt you'll also have friends who tried and failed to sell something in the past. But if you have an aggressive, driven personality, really believe in the product you are selling, and are willing to do the hard work it takes to network and be successful, you can make a home business out of it. Look at your social media accounts and see what your friends are selling, or if you have a friend who already sells a product you buy and love, ask how you can become a distributor. The bonus of taking on a business like this is that you won't just earn extra income, you can also get a significant discount on the product you are selling.

Work Extra Hours/Get Another Job

This is a no-brainer, but if you already have a part-time or full-time job, see if you can work extra hours to earn money for your Disney trip. A few hours of overtime a week can really add up. Volunteer to cover extra shifts for your coworkers.

If you like kids, let your friends and coworkers know you're available for babysitting. You can even put an ad (or answer ads) on sites like Care and Sitter City to find extra work, setting your own availability. These sites also let you sign up as a pet sitter, caregiver for the elderly, or home sitter. If you are good at teaching a subject like math, reading, or a foreign language, you can offer to tutor students. You can even become an online tutor using services like Skype. Try marketing your services on Tutor.com or on Craigslist.

There's also the possibility of getting another job just to earn vacation money, working nights or weekends at a store, restaurant, or food-delivery service. If you're 38 or younger, you might even consider joining a military Reserve unit. This is an especially good idea if you have prior service, since that service will count towards your attrition date in the Reserves. You must be willing to attend Basic Training and technical schools as required, and then serve one weekend a month and two weeks a year. There's also always the possibility that you could deploy. But you can get great benefits out of it, including insurance, college benefits, military discounts at Disney, and eligibility to stay at Shades of Green resort.

If you have a unique skill set, such as web design, app development, makeup artistry, bookkeeping, photography, writing, or fitness instruction, consider freelancing or starting a side business for extra income. Just make sure this is not going against the rules of your primary employer.

Take Stock Photos

If you enjoy photography, consider selling your images. Stock photography websites are always looking for images, and they pay; not very much, usually a few cents per image, but it can add up each time you sell a photo. And if you submit hundreds of photos, it can really add up. Check the submission guidelines at iStockPhoto and Shutterstock and always ensure you have the permission of any human subjects in your photos to use them in a stock photo. There's also an app called Foap that will do the same thing for iPhone photos.

Write or Blog

If you have a talent for writing or knowledge on any subject to share with others, consider writing freelance blog articles, journal articles, news articles, and other posts. Start a blog (but don't have unrealistic expectations about what you can earn). If you're not a writer but have something to share anyway, you could try starting a video blog on YouTube. If you decide to start a blog, be prepared to do some self-promotion in order to break into the saturated blogging market. Write a book; if it's too daunting to figure out how to get it published the old-fashioned way, self-publish through Amazon Kindle and set your own price. Amazon offers step-by-step instructions on how to do this on their site.

You can also be a freelance proofreader. The more you proofread, the more money you will make, so your income will depend on how efficiently you work. There's a free seven-day introductory course on how to proofread at Proofread Anywhere. The site is to help aspiring court transcriptionists, but the free course covers general proofreading skills.

Do Mystery Shops or Join Focus Groups

Here's one way to get paid in your spare time and sometimes get free stuff. During a mystery shop, you go to a store and either browse or complete a transaction. The mystery shop company usually gives you a script or guideline for what to do at the store. Then you must carefully evaluate the experience, noting every detail. The company will either pay you for your time, pay you back for merchandise you purchased, or both. Other mystery shop opportunities can include eating at restaurants and getting reimbursed for your meal and that of a guest, or test-driving cars and listening to the sales pitch. To avoid getting scammed, ensure the company you sign up with is a member of the MSPA, the organization that manages mystery-shopping companies. A listing of their member companies, with links to some of the companies' websites where you can sign up to be a shopper, is available on their website.

The app FieldAgent allows you to find secret-shopper tasks near you without signing up with a company. Once you accept a task, you have two hours to complete it.

QuickThoughts Missions and Mobee are apps that allow you to do secret shops for gift cards or cash.

There is even a way you can mystery shop at Disney and get a free ticket in return. Shoppers Critique International (a member of the MSPA) runs occasional mystery shopping opportunities for buying a Disney ticket at the gate, for which you will get reimbursed.

Focus groups are another relatively easy money-maker. The trick with these opportunities is that they are typically based in larger cities. Do a search to find legitimate focus group companies near you. Keep in mind that you should never pay a fee to find these companies.

Make and Sell Arts and Crafts

If you look at Etsy, people are making and selling just about anything you can think of, from art to clothing to soap to food. Now that Amazon has launched the Amazon Handmade marketplace, there is more than one place to sell your arts and crafts. Make sure you charge enough to make a profit after supplies and labor, but not so much that no one will buy what you have to sell. If anyone has ever said to you, "You could sell that on Etsy!" about something you've made, now is the time to take action.

Switch Banks or Start an Account

Some banks will give you a monetary incentive just for opening an account. At time of writing, I was hearing radio ads for a bank that was giving away a $150 Visa gift card for opening any type of account. Then I did an online search for "banks offering cash to open accounts" and found twenty similar current offers.

There's also an investment company called Stash that allows you to easily start a new investment account. Open an online account and download the app and the company will give you a $5 bonus. The app does charge $1 per month to cover their fees, so you'll want to invest more than that every month to make it worthwhile.

Open an account with the Clink app and save your money by investing $1 a day, or a percentage of the amount you spend dining out. If you do a search, you can find promo codes that will give you a bonus (usually $5) for opening an account.

Quit Smoking or Drinking

This one is probably obvious, but not only would it be good for your health to quit, you'd be saving a ton of money you could be putting into your Disney fund. Use an online calculator to figure out just how much you'd save. Friends of mine who've quit smoking say the resource that has helped them the most has been the book, "Allen Carr's Easy Way To Stop Smoking," available at online booksellers and bookstores everywhere.

On a related note, consider cutting down or out alcoholic beverages and see how much you will save. Just cutting out a $15 12-pack of beer every week would save $780 over the course of a year!

Lose Weight

Believe it or not, the site HealthyWage will pay you for losing weight. Just place a bet on how much you plan to lose. Then, stick to it! You won't get paid unless you lose the weight, but it could be that the thought of cash in your pocket will incentivize you to stick to your goal.

Become an Independent Contractor

Online independent-contractor service organizations are popping up seemingly overnight, with new ones out all the time. You can use an app to find someone willing to do just about anything for you, and on the flip side, these companies need people willing to do the work who don't necessarily want to be tied to a traditional corporate pay-and-benefits plan.

If you are over 21, have a clean driving record and spend a lot of time in your car, you might want to consider making some extra cash from it. When you sign up to be an Uber driver you will get to keep 80% of everything you earn as a driver and can set your own hours. You do need a four-door car. Don't forget about other ride-sharing services like Lyft or Via.

If you don't want to carry people in your car, you could consider signing up to be a shopper and delivery driver for a service like Instacart. If they're available near you, these services will pay you to shop for the items in a customer's grocery list and deliver them to their door. It's possible you could earn quite a bit if your customers are good tippers.

Have a spare room and don't mind the idea of a stranger in your house? Rent it out via AirBnB. I know several people who've had success doing this as a way to earn extra cash.

Sign up for Amazon's Mechanical Turk service and earn small amounts of cash (that add up) for doing simple tasks like proofreading. Amazon is also hiring delivery drivers in major cities under a new program called Flex.

Other sites where you can do small online tasks for pay are Fiverr, Fancy Hands, and Upwork. These are especially good sites to check out if you have experience with writing, editing, web design, or programming.

Test company websites or apps with UserTesting.

Apply to be a theatre checker with Certified Field Associates. This essentially means you can get paid to go to the movies! You can accept or decline as many assignments as you wish, and even pick and choose which assignments you're most interested in if there's a movie you particularly want to see. Your job might be to rate trailers or movies, discreetly count the number of people in attendance at a given showing, and performing mystery shops at theaters.

There are so many other services you can sign up to perform: examples are Handy for household services, Postmates for delivery, TaskRabbit for multiple kinds of freelance labor, DoorDash for food delivery, Washio for laundry and dry-cleaning, and new ones appearing all the time.

Full links to all these sites and services can be found in the Appendix.

Win the Lottery

It would be nice, wouldn't it? Unfortunately, statistics are against you on this one, but if you want to try, good luck!

In summary, no matter how you get extra money (or save money), be sure to pay it to yourself in your Disney fund. It may be slow going, but the more you put into it, the more you will get in return. And eventually you will earn the money you need to take the family vacation you've been dreaming about.

Chapter 8: Setting Aside Extra Money

While you're planning your Disney vacation, there are ways to cut the expense of the trip before you even go. Reducing the expense caused by booking transportation and lodging can make your dream vacation much more accessible. This can be done by making the vacation itself cheaper, or by reaching a savings goal that can be applied to the cost.

Pay Yourself First

Setting aside extra money without even feeling it is a great way to save up for Disney and reduce the burden of vacation expenses.

Save all your change! Don't spend any of it, and put it in a jar marked "Disney Money." Encourage your kids to donate to the jar, too! They may even look for odd jobs or start a lemonade stand to contribute. If you never spend your change, you will be amazed at how quickly you can accumulate hundreds of dollars without even noticing. Another trick is to "round up" all your spending, and contribute that amount to your fund. Did you spend $42.30 on something? Take the $0.70 it would take to make it an even amount and contribute that to your fund. You can look at your account on a daily or weekly basis, or write down the amount each time you make a transaction, and do the math on each expenditure.

Apps can help you start saving small amounts without noticing. Most charge a nominal fee for handling your money, like $1 a month. For example, instead of having to round up your spending by hand, an app called Acorns will automatically look at checks and bills you pay, round the number you paid up to the nearest dollar, and deposit the difference in an account. Other apps can make automatic deposits for you from one account into another so that it's easy to save money without even thinking about it. Examples are Digit and PlentyFi. Also check with your bank to see if you can set up an automatic transfer of a small amount that you can "set and forget."

For larger savings, you could stop spending $1 bills. Stash away any dollar bills you find into your Disney fund.

Contribute any "found money" like gifts, random cash found in the washing machine, coins you pick up on the street or find in your couch cushions, etc. to your Disney fund. Are you getting a tax refund that you could apply, all or in part, to your Disney fund? Get a small amount of cash back every time you go to the grocery store and add it to your fund.

Change Your Deductions

Do you get a tax refund every year? If so, you might want to change your deductions on your IRS form W4. This is the form you fill out at work to allow taxes to be deducted from your paycheck. Increasing the amount of deductions means you will get less money back in the form of a tax refund, but more money every paycheck to do with as you wish. That means more money in your Disney fund! Remember, a tax refund is your money; why are you loaning it to the government interest-free when you could be using it to earn interest towards your Disney vacation?

Refinance Your Mortgage

Have you thought about refinancing lately? Interest rates are still at record lows and you could possibly save hundreds of dollars every month. The Federal Reserve has published a handy guide on their website about refinancing. Most information on refinancing you will find through a search online will be on the websites of lenders, who will be trying to convince readers of the positives of refinancing; the Federal Reserve site will give you an unbiased overview.

If you are affording your monthly payments without any issues but find that you can refinance and lower your monthly payments, you could put the difference between the old and new payment in your Disney fund every month as a "no-pain" bonus until you reach your savings goal.

Try a Savings Challenge

There are also savings challenges you can participate in; for example, for every week of the year, you set aside some money. $1 in week 1, $2 in week 2, $3 in week 3, etc. all the way up to $52 in week 52. Or go downward from $52 by a dollar a week so you don't have to set aside as much when Christmastime nears. Saving this amount will net you $1,378 over a year. If this seems too daunting, you could set aside $1, $2, $3, etc. up to week $26, then repeat $26 the next week, then start going down as the weeks progress to $25, $24, $23 until you're back to $1 at the end of the year. Even that will net you $702 you wouldn't have saved otherwise. Another challenge involves setting aside $2 increments every week until you reach $52 mid-year ($2 the first week, $4 the second, $6 the third etc.) then repeating $52 one week and going down by $2 every week from there until the end of the year. If you follow this challenge, you will end up saving $1,404!

There are many other savings challenge ideas you can find online, or you can design your own challenge. For example, if you know you won't be going to Disney for a couple of years, you could spread your savings challenge out so that you are even less likely to feel an impact to your wallet. The point is that by setting aside a little money over time, you can find a painless way to make your savings add up.

Chapter 9: Reducing the Cost of your Vacation

Disney Gift Cards

Many people use Disney gift cards to fund their vacations. When you purchase these, be sure you are getting Disney gift cards that can be used at the parks rather than gift cards to the Disney store (Disney Gift Cards vs. Disney Store Gift Cards). If you're staying at a Disney resort, you can even use Disney gift cards to pay for your hotel. Disney gift cards are also a great way to help kids stick to a souvenir budget.

The trick to saving money by using Disney gift cards is to ensure you don't pay full price for them. Warehouse clubs often offer specials on gift cards; make sure to check on major sales holidays like Black Friday. Ask relatives and friends for Disney gift cards for holiday and birthday gifts. There are also gift card marketplaces and resellers like Raise where you can buy gift cards at a discount. Look for deals and coupons for these sites on other coupon sites and places like Swagbucks.

If you have a Target REDcard, you can get 5% off Disney gift cards by ordering them online. If you earn Target gift cards on sites like Swagbucks, you can use those gift cards to buy Disney gift cards on Target's site. If your REDcard is set to your default payment method, you can even get the 5% off even though you're paying with gift cards!

Fuel rewards programs and grocery store incentives (such as $10 off your bill with the purchase of any $50 gift card) are more ways to save on Disney gift cards.

Reward Points

If you or your spouse is a frequent traveler, you can check your hotel and airfare reward points and see if any of those can be used toward your Disney vacation. Be sure to check your credit cards for reward points, as well. With some cards, you may not have even realized you were accumulating points. Rewards points from credit cards and travel can be used to offset the cost of flights or hotel rooms, or can be used to pay for gift cards. If the rewards catalogue does not offer Disney gift cards, you could always get gift cards for places that sell Disney gift cards, like Target. You could also use them for gift cards to restaurants that are on or near Disney property, like Rainforest Café and Starbucks, or use them to pay for travel perks like your airport shuttle if you are not staying at a Disney resort. Some rewards programs like Citicard "Thank You" points can even enable you to purchase theme park tickets to Universal Studios and Disney World, but these require a lot of points and are not always available. If you are one who is excellent at paying off your credit cards every month, racking up points by putting all purchases on a card and then paying it off monthly could be one way to make a vacation more affordable.

Disney Credit Cards

If you know you can be disciplined with credit, there's the option of a Disney Visa card. There are two cards available, both from Chase: the Disney Rewards Card and the Disney Premier Card. Both cards allow you to rack up points toward Disney vacations and merchandise. The Premier Card offers more points per purchase (2%) but charges an annual fee of $49. The Rewards Card offers 1% of purchases back as points. Both cards offer other benefits such as a free character meet-and-greet with free photo on your vacation, 6 months of no interest when you book your Disney vacation with the card, and sometimes discounts and early access to vacation package specials.

There is also a Disney Visa Debit Card, but it does not offer points for purchases; it does offer some benefits like discounts and the same free character meet-and-greet and photo as the credit cards.

If you can manage credit well and think you might use a card enough to rack up significant points, you might want to compare the Rewards and Premier card and see which one would be a better option for you. If you're willing to pay the $49 fee to get the greater rewards of the Premier card, keep in mind that you'd have to spend over $4,900 in a year to reach that 2% level that would make it worthwhile over the no-fee Rewards card.

Although there might be a cachet about owning a Disney credit card, if you want to go the credit card route you might also want to investigate non-Disney-specific rewards cards like Discover or Chase Sapphire that will give you cash back or points at higher return rates than these cards. Watch out for annual fees; Discover doesn't have one, but Chase Sapphire charges $95 after the first year.

Chapter 10: Saving Money during Your Disney Vacation

So, you've managed to save up the money you need to go on vacation to Disney, and you've booked your trip. Congratulations! Now what?

Most people do have a set budget for their trip, and it would be a shame to arrive at Disney, throw that budget out the window in the interest of enjoying the "best vacation ever" and creating magical memories for their kids, and then have to come home and face bills they didn't expect. It's important to remember that while Disney is a magical place, in the end they are in the business of making money, and they want you to spend as much as possible while you are there.

Set Spending Limits

The easiest way to prevent overspending at Disney is to create a budget and stick to it. Be aware of how much you are spending. Without paying for everything with straight-up cash, this can be difficult to do. Disney has instituted a system where you can link your Magic Bands to a credit card and use them to charge food and merchandise back to your room (using a PIN code). Using this system it could be easy to let spending get out of hand. You don't have to use the Magic Bands to charge purchases, though. There are also mixed reports about whether or not you can set a spending limit for the bands for each PIN code that is established; check the My Disney Experience app to see if that's possible after you receive your bands.

Another way to keep track of spending is using Disney gift cards. If you have a budget you want to stick to and are planning on spending your time and money on Disney property during your trip, put that amount of money on a series of Disney gift cards. Each time you purchase something with a gift card, the receipt will show your remaining balance. This is a great way to give the kids some spending money while simultaneously teaching them money-management skills – hand them a Disney gift card, and away they go. Spent today's budget on that huge Mickey doll earlier in the day and now you can't get the Olaf doll you want? Too bad, so sad!

Do Free Things

Believe it or not, there are fun, free activities at Disney! These are especially rewarding if you have the self-control to browse without buying.

- Ride the monorail – the monorail is my toddler's favorite "ride," and is also enjoyed by my older child. There's something magical about getting to ride around in air-conditioned comfort, listening to the narration about the sites and locations, and just taking in the view of Disney World from the windows. There are three monorail routes you can take: an express from the Transportation and Ticket Center to the Magic Kingdom; a resort-hopper that stops at the Transportation and Ticket Center, the Polynesian Village Resort, the Grand Floridian Resort and Spa, the Magic Kingdom, and the Contemporary Resort; and a route that runs from the Transportation and Ticket Center to Epcot. The most fun route for children seems to be the resort-hopper, but they also enjoy the more extended ride to Epcot (especially when it circles Spaceship Earth and gives you a 360-degree view of Future World). There's no rule saying you have to get off, so you can stay and ride back and forth as long as you like.

- Ride the boats – just like the monorail, you don't have to be a guest at a Disney resort to ride the boats. You can go back and forth from the Transportation and Ticket Center to the Magic Kingdom, or from Disney's Hollywood Studios to the Boardwalk, Yacht Club, and Beach Club resorts, all for free.

- Explore the resorts – while you're monorail-hopping, it's fun to get out at some of the themed resorts and see how they're decorated. Check out the pool areas – they're for guests' use only, but are still fun to look at since they are designed so imaginatively. This can especially be fun around the holidays, when the resorts are decked out for Christmas. You can also explore the other Disney resorts by traveling there on the buses and boats. If you're driving, you can get a free 3-hour parking pass at each resort from the parking lot attendant; just tell them you're there to have a look around. Fun resorts to explore are the Boardwalk, Wilderness Lodge, and Animal Kingdom Lodge. Some of the resorts, like Animal Kingdom Lodge, offer free tours that you don't even need to be a guest to enjoy (try calling ahead and asking about tours). If you want to spend a little more money and are up for some grown-up entertainment, you could try to have a different signature drink at each resort. This is known as the monorail crawl!

Picture 7: Animal Kingdom Lodge

- Look for Hidden Mickeys – entire books have been
  written about the "hidden Mickeys" sprinkled all over
  Disney property. These are basically three circles
  configured to resemble Mickey Mouse's head.
  Children love going on spot-the-hidden-Mickey hunts,
  and it doesn't cost a thing. They can be found in the

resorts, theme parks, and even as a sand trap on the golf course.

- Visit Disney Springs – the newly renovated Disney Springs shopping complex offers a lot of opportunities for free entertainment. There are fountains to play in, street performers and live music, and even free Lego play areas at the Lego Imagination Center. Check the website for the Lego store for upcoming events there that may even include free mini model builds. Sometimes outside the chocolate stores and bakeries, workers hand out free samples.

- Watch a movie under the stars – the Fort Wilderness Campground and most of the other resorts offer variations on a campfire and Disney movie under the stars, free to all Disney resort guests. Fort Wilderness Campground usually sells s'mores kits, but you can also bring your own. The other resorts may even offer s'mores or marshmallows to roast for free! Make sure to call ahead or check with the resort, because these events could vary seasonally and due to weather.

- Watch the Electric Water Pageant – every night, a parade of boats covered in lights makes its way around the Magic Kingdom resort area. Check before you go to find out what time it will be running. You don't have to be a guest at the resorts to watch the pageant, just make your way to the dock or beach. These are also great locations from which to watch the nightly Magic Kingdom fireworks display for free!

- Free ice cream – if you attend a Disney Vacation Club presentation, they'll give you free ice cream at the end. Sure, you have to listen to all the reasons why investing in a Disney Vacation Club membership (timeshare) is wonderful, but they are much lower-pressure than traditional timeshare presentations. Basically, demand for the Disney Vacation Club is so high they don't need to pressure people to buy. So they'll tell you about it, and then give you free ice cream. You need to attend one of the scheduled presentations for this perk – check with any of the attendants at the Disney Vacation Club kiosks located all over the park and ask when you can listen to a presentation.

- Check out the amenities at your hotel or resort – wherever you are staying, there is likely to be a pool (or two, or more) where kids and adults can spend a happy afternoon without even going to the parks. Many resorts offer free activities and events – check with the staff when you check in to see what's going on during your stay.
- Free food and drink – if you're already in a Disney park, look for free samples, especially at bakeries and confectionaries. Epcot even offers Club COOL, an often-overlooked attraction that lets guests sample soda from around the world. The cups are small, but you can stand there and drink as much as you want. You can also ask for a cup of water at any Disney counter-service location, or any kiosk that sells fountain drinks, and receive one for free. A bottle of water was $2.50 in the park the last time I went, so there is definitely potential for savings there!
- Maps – park maps make great souvenirs, especially for the kids, and they're absolutely free!
- Disney planning DVD – prior to your trip, you can order a free planning DVD from Disney. It's a lot of fun to watch, and builds excitement for the trip for the whole family.

- Autographs – have your child bring a notebook or autograph book and fancy pen from home; you can even find Disney-themed ones at dollar stores. The Disney characters will be happy to sign their autograph book at every encounter, and it makes for a wonderful "free" souvenir.
- Buttons - Are you at Disney for a special occasion? Go to the Guest Services counter at the park and let them know. They'll give you a free button for the event, either customized for birthdays/anniversaries/honeymoon, or just says "I'm Celebrating!" Wearing these buttons around the park will also elicit congratulations and sometimes special treatment from cast members. Then you can keep the button as a fun souvenir!

Save Money on Food

There are lots of tips and tricks for saving money on your food budget. If you don't have the Disney Dining Plan, you especially have more leeway. Remember that the Disney Dining Plan is not necessarily a cheaper way to get meals; it's just already paid for.

The easiest way to save money on food is by eating breakfast in your room. Ensuring your room is equipped with a fridge and/or microwave helps a lot. Since my family brings our car, we always make a stop at a grocery store for food and snacks like milk, juice, muffins, fresh fruit, yogurt, and cereal. I pack disposable plates, bowls, and utensils from home, along with a roll of paper towels. The added benefit of this method is finishing our breakfast quickly and getting on to the fun instead of spending extra time in a restaurant. If you don't have access to a car, you can even get groceries delivered to your resort; check out We Go Shop, Garden Grocer, and other sites. Most hotels also have little grocery shops where you can purchase some basics; they will be more expensive than at a grocery store but less expensive than eating a meal in the park. If you have Amazon Prime, you can even use Prime Pantry to have a box of food and supplies delivered to the hotel for your arrival. Alternatively, flying an air carrier like Southwest that doesn't charge baggage fees can give you the freedom to pack extra food.

Although Disney does not allow large coolers into the parks (and who wants to drag a cooler around all day, anyhow?), it's a little-known fact that it does not prohibit bringing your own food to the parks. Making a picnic out of some peanut butter and jelly sandwiches can be a lot of fun. Also, consider carrying in snacks like individual baggies of chips, crackers, fruit gummies, granola bars, and nuts for when hunger strikes but you don't want to pay for an expensive snack. Just make sure that whatever you bring will not spoil in the Florida heat.

Drink the free ice water you can get at restaurants rather than buying bottled water or soda.

At counter service restaurants, adults can order kids' meals, or try to split an adult meal with another person. Sometimes they're enough food but sometimes they aren't, so have a walk through the dining area and scope out the serving sizes before ordering. Meal prices typically list a total that includes a side or sides and a drink; you can save by ordering the menu item without these extras, but you have to ask.

Eat a large late lunch around 1 or 2 in the afternoon, and then snack for dinner instead of ordering a whole meal. It should also be less crowded in the restaurants during a late lunch. And if you're at Disney during the hot season, it's much more pleasant to sit in an air-conditioned restaurant during the heat of the day than to walk from line to line in the sun. Meal prices also tend to be lower at lunchtime than at dinner.

Consider eating off property. There are chain restaurants, fast food, and delicious independent restaurants all within driving or cab/Uber distance from Disney property. Food delivery to your hotel room is another option that could end up being cheaper than eating at a table service restaurant in one of the parks. Check with sites like Groupon for deals at Disney-area restaurants. Use sites like Swagbucks and Perk to earn restaurant gift cards for places around Disney.

Bring or purchase alcohol and mixers to enjoy drinks in your hotel room instead of out at a bar. The price per drink will be much lower.

Save Money on Souvenirs

Paying for your theme park ticket, food, lodging, and transportation is just the beginning. Disney wants to entice you and your children to buy all kinds of wonderful souvenirs, too. There are shops and kiosks for this purpose on every corner of the World, it seems, and they are all full of wonderful and unique merchandise. By demonstrating some willpower, though, you can come away from your trip with great souvenirs that will keep you within your budget.

If you can manage to venture outside Disney property, you can find Disney's Character Warehouse outlets at two outlet malls nearby. These stores offer a very large assortment of authentic merchandise at discounted prices. One is at Orlando Vineland Premium Outlets right off Vineland Road outside Disney, and the other is in Orlando International Premium Outlets on the north end of International Drive. You'll want to check prices to ensure you really are getting a good deal, but as a rule they'll be much cheaper than the stores in the parks.

You can also find Disney merchandise at local big box retailers like Walmart, drugstores, and dollar stores. It may or may not be authentic, but it'll have your children's favorite characters on it and it will be cheap.

Another option is to think outside the box when it comes to souvenirs. Bring postcard stamps and let your children buy, write, and mail home postcards, or have characters autograph them. Bring an autograph book and pen from home and collect character autographs. If you've purchased the dining plan, you can use snack credits to buy packaged food and candy souvenirs from the shops. Use your camera to take lots of photo souvenirs instead of buying things. When you get home, you can use your photos to create inexpensive mementos from photo gallery sites like Shutterfly, CafePress, and Zazzle.

You can even get souvenirs before you leave home. Dollar stores are great locations to get Disney-themed small toys, books, puzzles, and other trinkets that can be handed out at the parks whenever the kids are clamoring for an expensive souvenir. They are also a wonderful place to get glow-in-the-dark necklaces, bracelets, and other toys, which you can hand out during the wait for the nighttime parade or fireworks when there are lots of vendors around tempting your kids with pricey glow-in-the-dark and light-up toys. I did this for my kids recently and they were perfectly content to get the dollar store toys instead of shelling out for official souvenirs.

Your children may enjoy collecting pressed pennies as souvenirs. Pressed penny machines are all over the parks and resorts, and cost $0.50 plus a shiny penny. The penny is stamped into a souvenir disc you can keep as a memento of your visit.

Collecting and trading pins can also be an inexpensive activity that results in fun souvenirs. For a small investment in a starter bag of pins (less than $20), your kids can find cast members and other guests willing to trade and exchange pins during the trip.

If you are visiting during one of the hotter times of the year, keep in mind that one of the most in-demand souvenirs at these times is the portable battery-powered misting fan. They sell for around $20 in the parks, but they can be found much cheaper before you go, either at big box discount stores or online at places like Amazon. If you want to get them for the kids you could even give them a pack of Disney stickers from the dollar store and let them decorate their own fans. Lanyards are a great way to carry the fans around once you're in the park. Don't forget batteries, and you may want to check and see if you will need a small screwdriver to open the battery compartment to the fan.

Here's a tip if your little princess is clamoring for a makeover at Bibbidi Bobbidi Boutique, either at Magic Kingdom or Disney Springs. There are different levels of pricing for the makeovers, which include additional items like a sash and a princess dress. The difference between the lowest level makeover and the makeover that includes a Disney princess dress, crown, and wand is about $150. You can buy these accessories online before your trip (try Amazon) for under $20. Your little girl can arrive at her makeover already dressed up like a princess, and you can save a bundle.

Stroller Rentals

If you have younger children, you may want to consider renting a stroller instead of bringing your own. Strollers are available to rent at the theme parks themselves for $15 a day or $13 a day for a multi-day stay. Double strollers are available for $31 a day or $27 a day for a multi-day stay. Not only is this expensive, I've also read that the Disney strollers are uncomfortable for children and unwieldy to steer. In addition, when you ride certain rides you'll have to leave your stroller in a stroller parking area – and then return and spend valuable time trying to figure out which of the many identical strollers is yours.

A better option is to rent a stroller from a private stroller rental company. There are several to choose from, and most of these companies will deliver your stroller right to your hotel. Prices vary from much cheaper than Disney to much more expensive than Disney. You'll have to do some price comparisons to make sure you're getting the best deal. Don't forget to search for online coupon codes!

Another option is to bring a very cheap folding umbrella stroller or buying one when you're in the Orlando area just for your trip. These can be had for less than $20 at large discount stores. You can even choose to have it shipped to your hotel.

Do You Need Memory Maker?

Disney's PhotoPass is the name of the service provided where photographers stationed all over the parks and resorts take your picture. You can purchase the photographs individually, but are under no obligation to purchase any photos. It's handy for making sure everyone in your family gets in the picture, and there are photo stops in front of all the major landmarks like Cinderella's Castle and Spaceship Earth. PhotoPass also includes photos taken during character dining and on rides. You can even add borders and animation to some PhotoPass photos. The photos are sharp, crisp, and high-quality.

Disney also offers a service called Memory Maker that allows you unlimited digital access to all the photographs taken with PhotoPass during your trip. The main downside is the price. You can pre-pay for this service before your trip, if you know you'll want it, for $149. If you decide you want Memory Maker while you're already on your trip, it will cost $169. Whether you want to pay for the service or not depends entirely on your personal preference – how many pictures do you plan to take with the whole family? Do you like collecting photos of your family on rides, for example? Do you want to stop in front of all the scenic views and get family photos taken? It is also nonrefundable, so if you decide during your trip that you haven't taken enough photos to get your money's worth, you're out of luck.

In the past, there have been ways to get around Disney's encryption and download any and all PhotoPass photos for free, but it looks as though Disney is now cracking down on these methods. You can still take a screenshot of any PhotoPass pictures during your 30-day viewing period, but it will be much lower resolution than the photo you will receive upon purchase.

If you still want great pictures of your family but don't want to purchase them, I've read that the cast members who take PhotoPass photos will use your own camera or phone to take the same picture if you ask nicely. There's also the old-fashioned option of asking a stranger to take a photo of your family. Most people are happy to do this, especially if you offer to take one of them in return. Approach people taking selfies; with the banning of selfie sticks at Disney parks, people are usually happy to get a photo of themselves from further away than arm's length.

Chapter 11: Yes, You Can Afford Disney!

A Disney vacation can be expensive. Recent news articles and data from the Orlando Tourism Bureau have estimated that the average household income of a family going to Disney World is over $90,000[4]. Disney ticket prices continue to increase year-by-year. There are several reasons for this; despite the higher prices, attendance shows no sign of dropping, indicating that Disney has no incentive to keep prices the same or less. As a business, Disney also takes the line that if it is *too* affordable, the crowds will be unmanageable and the average guest experience will drop to unacceptable levels. Disney is even offering more and more upgraded and premium experiences for extra fees, showing their willingness to continue to cater to the higher-income customer. If you're trying to book a vacation without careful budgeting and planning ahead, even a basic Disney vacation will be well out of reach for most families without going into serious debt.

---

[4] "How theme parks like Disney World left the middle class behind," The Washington Post, June 12, 2015 https://www.washingtonpost.com/news/business/wp/2015/06/12/how-theme-parks-like-disney-world-left-the-middle-class-behind/

"As Disney World Tickets Break $100, There Are Signs Disney Vacations Are Now Only for the Rich," Frommers.com, February 22, 2015 http://www.frommers.com/community/blogs/arthur-frommer-online/_ticket-disney-world-passes-100-mark-disney-vacations-now-only-rich

"Disney breaks the $100 ticket barrier," Orlando Sentinel, February 22, 2015 http://www.orlandosentinel.com/travel/attractions/the-daily-disney/os-disney-tickets-100-20150222-story.html

What would Walt say? I think that he envisioned Disney World as a place all children could go to make magical memories. In that spirit, let's make sure Disney doesn't have to be a playground just for the wealthy. Using the tips in this book, with enough careful planning and preparation, anyone can afford to take their family to Disney and create memories that will last a lifetime, without breaking the bank.

Appendix: Online Resources

Here I've accumulated a list of some websites and blogs you may find very helpful in your quest to make Disney affordable. This list is by no means exhaustive, and a simple search engine query can help you find hundreds of other great articles and sources of information. Websites change frequently, so also keep in mind that it was up-to-date as of August-September 2016. It's in alphabetical order, so no site is recommended over any other site. They're all great resources.

Disney's Official Site
https://disneyworld.disney.go.com

Disney-Specific Money-Saving Sites
https://www.chase.com/online/Credit-Cards/disney.htm - Disney Rewards Credit Cards by Chase
http://www.couponingtodisney.com/ - tips for saving money for Disney
http://www.disboards.com/forums/budget-board.22/ - tips for saving money for Disney
https://disneyvacationaccount.disney.go.com/ - information about the Disney vacation account
https://disneyworld.disney.go.com/florida-residents/ - discounts for Florida residents
http://www.frugaltravelguy.com/?s=Disney - tips for saving money for Disney
https://www.getawaytoday.com/ - discount ticket broker
http://www.mapleleaftickets.com/ - discount ticket broker
http://www.militarydisneytips.com/ - discount information for the military
http://www.mousesavers.com/- tips for saving money for Disney

http://www.themouseforless.com/ - tips for saving money for Disney

https://parksavers.com/ - discount ticket broker

http://thepointsguy.com/category/disney/ - tips for saving money for Disney

http://pointsandpixiedust.boardingarea.com/ - tips for saving money for Disney

https://www.undercovertourist.com/ - discount ticket broker

General Money-Saving and Budgeting Sites

https://www.dailyworth.com/ - general money-saving advice

http://energy.gov/energysaver/lighting-choices-save-you-money - tips on saving money on electricity

http://frugalliving.about.com/ - general money-saving advice

http://thekrazycouponlady.com/ - general money-saving advice

http://www.livingonadime.com/ - general money-saving advice

https://www.mint.com/ - budgeting app

https://www.mvelopes.com/ - budgeting app

http://www.mymoneyblog.com/ - general money-saving advice

http://www.pinterest.com/ - search site for frugal living, recipes, crafts, travel, etc.

http://www.stretcher.com/ - general money-saving advice

http://www.thepennyhoarder.com/ - general money-saving advice

http://www.thesimpledollar.com/ - general money-saving advice

https://www.youneedabudget.com/ - budgeting app

Travel Money-Saving Sites

https://www.airbnb.com/ - vacation rental by owner

http://www.airfarewatchdog.com/fare-alerts/ - airfare price tracker
http://www.autodriveaway.com/ - drive someone else's car
http://www.expedia.com/ - vacation booking
http://www.farecompare.com/- airfare price tracker
http://www.theflightdeal.com/ - cheap fare finder
http://www.frugaltravelguy.com/ - general travel money-saving information
http://www.gasbuddy.com/ - real-time gas station pricing
http://www.hopper.com/ - airfare price tracker
https://www.hotels.com/ - vacation booking
https://www.hoteltonight.com/ - last-minute vacation booking
https://www.hotwire.com/ - vacation booking
https://www.kayak.com/ - vacation booking
http://koa.com/campgrounds/kissimmee/ - campground near Disney
https://www.lyft.com/ - ride-sharing site
http://www.orbitz.com/travel-deals/flight-deals/ - vacation booking
http://thepointsguy.com/ - general travel money-saving information
https://www.priceline.com/ - vacation booking
https://www.skyscanner.com/ - airfare price tracker
http://www.secretflying.com/ - cheap fare finder
http://www.smartertravel.com - general travel money-saving information
https://www.travelocity.com/ - vacation booking
http://www.trivago.com - hotel metasearch site
https://www.uber.com/ - ride-sharing site
https://www.vrbo.com/ - vacation rentals by owner
https://www.waze.com/ - real-time directions and gas station pricing

Disney and Travel Planning Information
http://www.allears.net/ - Disney planning information

http://www.BetterBidding.com – hotel bidding (Priceline and Hotwire) tips and information

http://www.disboards.com/ - the forums for wdwinfo.com

http://www.disneyfoodblog.com/ - Disney dining information

http://www.disneydining.com/ - Disney dining information

http://www.doctordisney.com/ - Disney planning information

https://www.disneyplanning.com/ - official Disney planning information site (free DVD)

https://eatingwdw.com/ - Disney dining information

http://floridasturnpike.com/TollCalcV5/index.htm

http://www.gardengrocer.com/ - Disney area grocery delivery service

https://www.google.com/maps/ - travel and routing information

http://www.kayak.com/ - travel planning information

http://www.intercot.com/ - Disney planning information

http://stores.lego.com/en-us/stores/us/orlando - Lego store at Disney Springs

https://www.mouseplanet.com/ - Disney planning information

http://www.premiumoutlets.com/outlet/orlando-international - outlet mall with Disney's Character Warehouse

http://www.premiumoutlets.com/outlet/orlando-vineland - outlet mall with Disney's Character Warehouse

https://touringplans.com/ (Subscription access, but free information available as well. If you decide to subscribe, search for a coupon code first.)

https://www.tripadvisor.com/ - general travel planning

http://www.wdwinfo.com/ - Disney planning information

http://www.wdwmagic.com/ - Disney planning information

http://wdwprepschool.com/ - Disney planning information

http://www.wegoshop.com/ - Disney area grocery delivery service

Apps and Websites for Making and Saving Money

https://www.acorns.com/ - automatic saving app

http://www.amazon.com - sell books, miscellaneous sales

https://www.bing.com/rewards/dashboard - gift card earning site

https://bookscouter.com/ - books

http://www.boxed.com/invite/OFKHJ - groceries and household goods

http://www.buffaloexchange.com/ - sell clothing

http://www.cafepress.com/ - photo printing and gift site

http://camelcamelcamel.com/ - Amazon price tracking site

http://www.cashinmybag.com/ - sell clothing

http://www.cashyourlaptop.com/ - sell laptops, cell phones, tablets

https://www.chase.com/online/Credit-Cards/disney.htm - rewards credit cards

https://www.checkout51.com/ - grocery cash back app

https://www.choosemyplate.gov/budget-create-grocery-game-plan - tips for eating healthy on a budget

https://www.choosemyplate.gov/lets-talk-trash - tips for not wasting food

https://www.citi.com/credit-cards/compare-credit-cards/citi.action?ID=thank-you-rewards-credit-cards – rewards credit cards

https://clink.com/ - investing site

http://www.clothesmentor.com/ - sell clothing

http://www.cnet.com/ - software reviews

http://www.coolfreebielinks.com/ - samples and freebies

http://www.coolserialnumbers.com - check for collectable money

http://www.coupons.com - discounts and coupons

http://www.couponsherpa.com/ - discounts and coupons

http://www.craigslist.org/about/sites - miscellaneous sales

https://creditcards.chase.com/a1/sapphire/compare - rewards credit card

https://www.decluttr.com/ - sell CDs, DVDs, games

https://digit.co/ - automatic saving app
http://www.directtextbook.com/ - sell books
https://www.discover.com/ - rewards credit card
https://disneydebit.com/ - rewards debit card
http://www.ebay.com/ - miscellaneous sales
http://www.ebates.com/ - cash back and discounts on online purchases
http://www.emeals.com/ - meal planning site
https://www.groupon.com/ - coupons and discount codes
http://www.federalreserve.gov/pubs/refinancings/default.htm - consumer guide to refinancing
http://www.financialcalculator.org/personal-finance/stop-smoking-calculator - savings calculator for smoking cessation
http://www.freecycle.com/ - buy/sell/trade, but all items are free
https://www.flipp.com/ - sale price comparison app
http://www.gamestop.com/ - sell CDs, DVDs, Games
https://www.gazelle.com/ - sell cell phones
https://www.getslidejoy.com/ - cash for having an ad on your phone lock screen
http://get.viggle.com/ - gift card earning site
http://www.goodrx.com/ - prescription information
http://www.groceryiq.com/ - grocery planning app
https://healthywage.com/ - earn money for losing weight
https://www.healthwarehouse.com/ - save money on prescriptions
https://ibotta.com/ - grocery cash back app
http://www.iheartkroger.com/ - tips for saving money at Kroger
http://www.i-say.com/ - gift card earning site (surveys)
https://us.letgo.com/en - miscellaneous sales
https://www.loanables.com/ - rent out your things
https://www.mobisave.com/ - grocery cash back app
https://www.mobilexpression.com/Home.aspx - earn money for having your online activity tracked

https://www.mypoints.com/emp/u/index.vm - gift card earning site

https://www.ncponline.com/panel/US/EN/Login.htm - gift card earning site

https://offerupnow.com/ - miscellaneous sales

http://www.onavo.com/ - cell phone data savings app

https://paribus.co/i/D4Jmlr - cash back for online purchases

http://perk.fm/4uiyn - gift card earning site

https://plentyfi.com/ - automatic saving app

https://poshmark.com/ - sell clothing

https://www.quickthoughtsapp.com/ - gift card earning site

https://www.raise.com/buy-gift-cards - discount gift cards

http://receipthog.com/ - grocery cash back app

http://repairpal.com/ - car repair estimate comparisons

http://www.retailmenot.com – discount codes and coupons

http://www.rewardtv.com/ - TV trivia

https://savingstar.com/ - grocery cash back app

http://www.sbkcenter.com/consumer_panelist_pop_c.php - junk mail buyer

http://www.secondspin.com/ - sell CDs, DVDs, games

https://www.sellcell.com/ - sell cell phones

http://shopkick.com/ - rebate app

https://www.shopmium.com/ - grocery cash back app

http://www.shopyourway.com/ - rebate site

https://www.shutterfly.com/ - photo printing and gift site

https://www.skype.com/en/ - free phone calls

https://www.sling.com/ - cheaper TV viewing

http://www.snipsnap.it/ - coupons and discount codes

https://www.stashinvest.com/ - investing app

https://www.stylelend.com/ - sell clothing

https://www.surveyspot.com/ - gift card earning site (surveys)

http://www.swagbucks.com/refer/mmb10863 - gift card earning site

https://targettrade-in.com/online/home/index.rails – Target buy-back for games and electronics

https://www.thredup.com/ - sell clothing
http://www.totallytarget.com/ - tips for saving money at Target
https://vertosmart.com/ - earn money for having your online activity tracked
http://www.vipvoice.com/ - survey site for earning gift cards
http://wildforcvs.com/ - tips for saving money at CVS
http://www.zazzle.com/ - photo printing and gift site

Side Job Opportunities

https://www.airbnb.com/host - accommodation rental service
https://services.amazon.com/handmade/handmade.htm - handmade arts and crafts
https://app.fieldagent.net/ - mystery shopping
http://www.autodriveaway.com/ - vehicle relocating service
https://www.care.com/ - child/home/pet/elder sitting services
https://www.certifiedfieldassociate.com/ - theatre checks
http://www.craigslist.org/about/sites - miscellaneous jobs and services
https://www.doordash.com/ - meal delivery service
http://drivewithvia.com/ – driving service (NYC and Chicago)
http://www.etsy.com – handmade arts and crafts
https://www.fancyhands.com/ - freelance online small jobs
https://www.fiverr.com/ - freelance online small jobs
https://flex.amazon.com/ - Amazon delivery drivers
https://www.foap.com/ - stock photo purchasing
https://www.getwashio.com/ - laundry and dry-cleaning delivery service
https://www.handy.com/ - cleaning and home services
http://www.istockphoto.com/ - stock photo purchasing
https://kdp.amazon.com/ - Kindle ebook publishing guidelines
https://www.lyft.com/drivers/ - driving service

http://mobeeapp.com/ - mystery shopping

http://www.mspa-na.org/member-companies - Mystery shopping companies

https://www.mturk.com/ - small computer task service

https://postmates.com/ - delivery service

https://proofreadanywhere.com/ - proofreading starter course

https://www.quickthoughtsapp.com/ - mystery shopping

https://www.shopperscritique.com/ - mystery shopping

https://shoppers.instacart.com/ - grocery shopping and delivery service

http://www.shutterstock.com/ - stock photo purchasing

https://www.sittercity.com/ - child/home/pet/elder sitting services

https://www.taskrabbit.com/ - miscellaneous job service

http://www.tutor.com/ - tutoring services

https://www.uber.com/drive/ - driving service

https://www.upwork.com/ - freelance proofreading, writing/editing, web design

https://www.usertesting.com/ - testing websites and apps

About the Author

Michelle Crawford has lived in Florida for nearly three-quarters of her life, including a ten-year stint in Orlando itself. At one point she lived in an apartment so close to the Magic Kingdom she could see and hear the fireworks every evening from her balcony. Though she now lives in the panhandle, she enjoys visiting Disney World as often as possible and is discovering the joys of introducing her children to the magic of Disney. She works as a computer scientist, but uses many of the tips in this book to fund her vacations.